VOICES FOUND

Church Publishing, New York

Musical autography by Music Graphics International

Church Publishing Incorporated
19 East 34th Street
New York, NY 10016

Copyright information will be found on page 263.

5 4

Preface

Voices Found: Women in the Church's Song is a rich collection of hymns and spiritual songs by, for, and about women. Overall, the music is written in congregational hymn style and is intended for use in the average parish church. There is also historical material and music arranged for women's voices. There are texts most appropriate for women's conferences and for children's informal activities, as this book seeks to expand the concept of congregational singing.

The goals of *Voices Found* are:

1. To affirm women's quest for spiritual and social justice
2. To broaden the repertoire of music available to the church
3. To continue a tradition of excellence in congregational singing

The international committees that produced this volume decided that a search for excellence was paramount. The first presentation of women's sacred music needed to reflect the very best texts and music available; thus, the review process was lengthy and inclusive. The result has been the discovery of a wealth of materials, new and old, that will enrich every parish with the voices of women.

In 1995, just after the twentieth anniversary of the ordination of women to the priesthood in the Episcopal Church, a group of laywomen at St. Mark's Church, Locust Street, in Philadelphia, began to meet regularly to encourage each other to find their voices in worship. The music and liturgy of the church had only begun to reflect women's needs. With the approval of the Rev. Charles Moore, rector, the group worshiped monthly in the Lady Chapel using newly authorized supplemental liturgical texts. They wanted to sing music by women, but found little in *The Hymnal 1982*. Lisa Neufeld Thomas, organist for the service, began searching for resources. Newer hymnals contained somewhat more music representative of women, but it became clear that a focused effort to collect and commission such music was needed—songs about women saints, women in scripture, and churchwomen. Everyone needed to learn about women's contributions to sacred song throughout history, to learn about our foremothers. Women needed role models in spiritual, liturgical, and musical leadership.

With the sponsorship of bishops Allen Bartlett, Barbara Harris, Frank Griswold, and John Howe, the following resolution was passed by the 1997 General Convention of the Episcopal Church:

Resolved, That the 72nd General Convention commends the Standing Commission on Church Music for its efforts toward preparing a supplement to the Hymnal 1982; and be it further

Resolved, That the Standing Commission on Church Music be directed to prepare an additional supplement which emphasizes liturgical music, hymns and other songs by women composers and poets both historical and contemporary; texts and music to be included which celebrate the contributions and diversity of women in scripture, women saints and churchwomen; and be it further

Resolved, That the sum of $25,000 be appropriated in the General Convention budget of the triennium 1998-2000 for the preparation of this supplement.

Unfortunately, the funding requested was not appropriated.

The Board of Directors of the Women's Sacred Music Project, an incorporated public charity which had grown out of the experience at St. Mark's, proceeded as agents for the Standing Commission on Church Music (now known as the Standing Commission on Liturgy and Music) in compiling this hymnal. They were assisted by the communications office of the Diocese of Pennsylvania and given work space by Rosemont College. An ecumenical group of women, who volunteered their time and expenses, developed a review process for the overwhelming number of submissions.

Review Committee

The Rev. Virginia Doctor
The Rt. Rev. Carol Gallagher
Dr. Gail Ramshaw
Dr. Virginia Ratigan

The Rt. Rev. Catherine Roskam
Lisa Neufeld Thomas, Convener
The Rev. Paula Wehmiller

Subsequently some funding was provided from the Congregational Ministries budget at the Episcopal Church Center, the Rev. Winston Ching, Director.

A text committee reviewed submissions looking for texts that:

· address women in scripture
· celebrate women saints and churchwomen
· reflect racial and ethnic diversity with sensitivity
· highlight the history of women in sacred song
· provide expansive imagery for God
· prove appropriate for congregational use

Text Committee

The Rt. Rev. Allen Bartlett
The Rev. Dr. Robert W. Carlson
The Rev. Dr. Lynn Collins
Sr. Élise, CHS
Barbara Fairfax
The Rt. Rev. Carol Gallagher

Sr. Helena-Marie, CHS
Ana Hernández
Dr. Virginia Ratigan
Blandina Salvador
Lisa Neufeld Thomas, Convener

A user group of clergy, musicians, and "women in the pew" reviewed submissions looking for texts that were:

- approachable by the average congregation
- reflective of a diversity of styles
- able to be performed with a flexible keyboard accompaniment
- representative of women's contribution to sacred music throughout history

User Advisory Group

The Rt. Rev. Allen Bartlett
Jonathan Bowen
Judith Dodge
Sr. Élise, CHS
Gary Fitzgerald
Dr. Carl Haywood
Christopher Helyer
Christopher Johnson
The Rev. Charles Moore

Henrietta Morgan
The Rt. Rev. Vincent Pettit
Dr. Virginia Ratigan
Dr. Barry Rose
Blandina Salvador
The Rev. Paulette Schiff
Margaret Schneider
Lisa Neufeld Thomas, Convener
Tom Whittemore

Finally, an editorial committee reviewed both texts and music and determined the final shape of the supplement. It was apparent that hymns, psalms, canticles, and spiritual songs were the strongest submissions.

Editorial Committee

Judith Dodge
Gary Fitzgerald
Dr. Carl Haywood
The Rt. Rev. Vincent Pettit
Lisa Neufeld Thomas, Convener

This book is a unique compilation of contemporary and historical materials that crosses boundaries of geography, time, and culture as it represents the diversity of the gifts of women. It is the hope of the committees that this innovative collection of music will affirm and expand the spirituality of all women and men as they find new voices in the church's song.

Publisher's Note

A Leader's Guide is available which duplicates the contents of this book and contains background information about each selection, performance notes, additional accompaniment parts and suggestions for the liturgical use of the music.

Church Publishing would like to acknowledge with gratitude the editorial assistance of J. Michael Roush in the preparation of this book.

Other hymnals and supplements available from Church Publishing are

The Hymnbook 1982
El Himnario
Lift Every Voice and Sing II
Wonder, Love, and Praise

http://www.churchpublishing.org

Table of Contents

Indices

Holy woman, graceful giver

1 Ho - ly wo-man, grace-ful giv - er, pro - phet, ser - vant, and be-liev - er,
2 Like the ves-sel, we are bro-ken; like the oint-ment, we are to - ken
3 In these jars is hid - den trea-sure, cost - ly fra - grance, Christ-ly plea-sure,
4 Ho - ly wo-man, cost - ly trea-sure, with the jar of al - a-bas - ter

wo - man with the oint - ment jar, rose up near the time ap - point - ed
of God's lov - ing un - to death; like the wo - man, we are ser - ving;
like the Christ, first from the dead, bro - ken for cre - a - tion's whole-ness,
shows the hid - den gift we are, there-fore let us as Christ's ser - vants

broke the seal, Christ's head a - noint-ed for the com-ing fa - tal hour.
like the scold-ers, ill de-serv-ing such a rich, for-giv-ing faith.
poured out for its com-ing full - ness, pro-phet ser - vant, hope and head.
hold our sis - ter in re-mem-brance—wo-man with the oint - ment jar.

Myrrh-bearing Mary

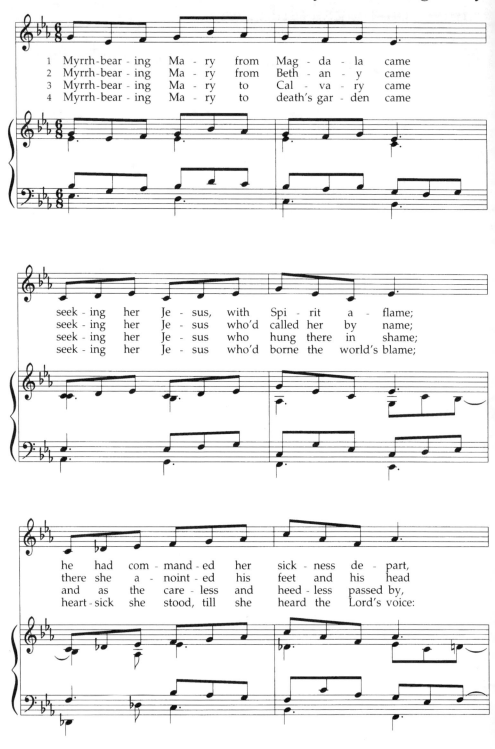

1 Myrrh-bear - ing Ma - ry from Mag - da - la came
2 Myrrh-bear - ing Ma - ry from Beth - an - y came
3 Myrrh-bear - ing Ma - ry to Cal - va - ry came
4 Myrrh-bear - ing Ma - ry to death's gar - den came

seek - ing her Je - sus, with Spi - rit a - flame;
seek - ing her Je - sus who'd called her by name;
seek - ing her Je - sus who hung there in shame;
seek - ing her Je - sus who'd borne the world's blame;

he had com - mand - ed her sick - ness de - part,
there she a - noint - ed his feet and his head
and as the care - less and heed - less passed by,
heart - sick she stood, till she heard the Lord's voice:

she   now   would   thank   him   for   new   -   ness ___   of
with   pre - cious   oils   that   were   meant   for ___   the
hope - less   and   help - less   she   watched   her ___   Lord
"Ma - ry!"   he   said,   "I   am   ris - en; ___   re   -

1.–3.

heart.
dead.
die.

1.–3.

4.

joice!" _____

4.

3   Verbum bonum

Translation
Let us sound out the word pure and sweet,
that Ave, through which the virgin, a mother's daughter,
became the chamber of Christ.
that Ave, mother of the true Solomon, fleece of Gideon,
whose childbirth the magi praised with three gifts.
Ave, you who bore Daylight;
Ave, you brought forth an offspring into a fallen world
you brought life and order.
Ave, bride of the highest Word,
safe harbour from the sea
sign in the thornbush
source of fragrant incense, mistress of angels,
amend us we plea
and amended, commend us to your son
that we might have eternal joy.

Mary heard the angel's message

1 Ma - ry heard the an - gel's mess - age:
2 When she heard her cou - sin's greet - ing,
3 Ma - ry heard the shep - herds' sto - ry,
4 Ma - ry heard, "Who is my moth - er?
5 When they learned the Lord had ris - en,

"Greet - ings Ma - ry, fa - vored one.
Ma - ry's heart was filled with joy,
words she trea - sured with de - light.
Who is in my fa - mi - ly?
Christ's dis - ci - ples met to pray.

Do not fear, for God____ is with____ you;
so she sang of God's____ great bless - ing
Then an an - gel gave____ the warn - ing:
All who do my Fa - ther's bid - ding,
Ma - ry was a - mong____ the faith - ful,

Em   Am7   Em   D

"May   it   be   as   you   have   spok - en;
God   has   worked,   the   proud   to   scat - ter;
Flee - ing   then,   she   held   him   close - ly.
You,   my   friend,   be - hold   your   moth - er!"
Like   her,   may   we   hear   and   an - swer,

G   Am   C   D   Em

I'm   the   ser - vant   of   the   Lord!"
hum - ble,   hung - ry   ones   to   raise."
One   day   she   would   let   him   go.
So   Christ   formed   new   bonds   of   care.
"We,   your   ser - vants,   live   for   you."

I am he for whom you long

1 "I am he   for whom you long,   the One   you   most de-sire."
2 "I am God: See! From   my   works   I   ne-ver   lift   my hand."
3 "This I say   is   so   great bliss: that we   should be   his crown!"

With these words our   court-eous Lord   set Ju - li - an   on fire.
With these words our   court-eous Lord   re - vealed what he   or - dained.
With these words Dame Ju - li - an   be - gan   to   write it   down.

In   fall - ing and   in   ris - ing   we are   kept __ pre - cious-ly.

All   shall   be well   and shall be   well for all e - ter - ni - ty.

Loud are the bells of Norwich

1 Loud are the bells of Nor-wich and the peo - ple come and go,
2 Love, like a yel - low daf - fo - dil, is com-ing through the snow.
3 Ring for the yel - low daf - fo - dil, the flow - er in the snow.

here by the tower of Jul - i - an I tell them what I know.
Love, like a yel - low daf-fo - dil is Lord of all I know.
Ring for the yel - low daf-fo-dil and tell them what I know.

Refrain

Ring out, bells of Nor-wich, and let the win - ter

Last time to Coda

come and go: all shall be well a - gain, I know.

Words and Music: Sydney Carter © 1981 Stainer and Bell Ltd. (admin. Hope Publishing Company,
Carol Stream, IL 60188); acc. Carl Haywood; bell acc., Linda Wilberger Egan. All rights reserved. Used by permission.
You must contact Hope Publishing Company to reproduce this selection.

We sing our praise of Hildegard

1 We sing our praise of Hil-de-gard, a wo-man for all time;
2 We now af-firm with Hil-de-gard we do not live a-lone,
3 We praise the joy that Hil-de-gard found in God's con-stant care.
4 We ce-le-brate with Hil-de-gard the green-ing of the soul.

a pro-phe-tess who ur-ges us to seek the light di-vine.
but are a part of all that is: each tree, each bird, each stone.
She trust-ed God to car-ry her, a fea-ther born on air.
The mois-ture from the Spi-rit's breath can cleanse us, make us whole.

Her vis-ion came in-sis-tent-ly, sent by her Liv-ing Light.
All crea-tures sing cre-a-tion's praise; yet we a-lone pos-sess
May such a faith in-spi-rit us, give us a breath-ing space,
May we now share life-giv-ing love, help jus-tice find a home,

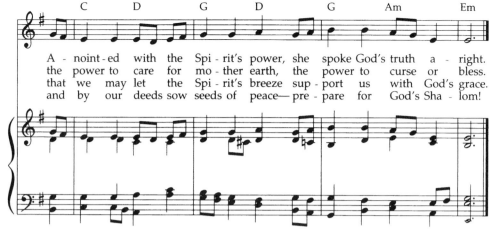

A - noint-ed with the Spi - rit's power, she spoke God's truth a - right.
the power to care for mo - ther earth, the power to curse or bless.
that we may let the Spi - rit's breeze sup - port us with God's grace.
and by our deeds sow seeds of peace— pre - pare for God's Sha - lom!

Keyboard and guitar should not sound together.

Words: Edith Sinclair Downing © 1995 Edith Sinclair Downing. All rights reserved. Used by permission.
Music: *Kingsfold*, English melody; adapt. Ralph Vaughn Williams © Oxford University Press. All rights reserved.
         Used by permission.
You must contact Oxford University Press to reproduce this music.

Miserere miseris 8

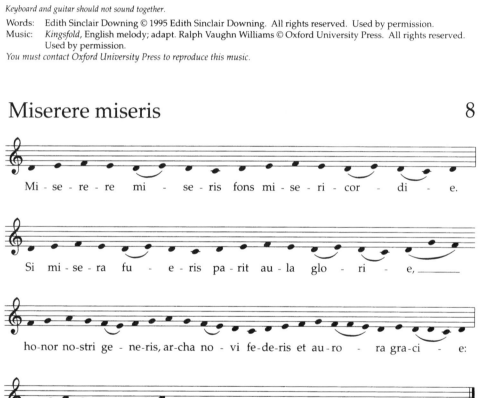

Mi - se - re - re mi - se - ris fons mi - se - ri - cor - di - e.

Si mi - se - ra fu - e - ris pa - rit au - la glo - ri - e, _____

ho - nor no - stri ge - ne - ris, ar - cha no - vi fe - de - ris et au - ro - ra gra - ci - e:

cer - te si vo - lu - e - ris, o be - nig - na po - te - ris da - re lo - cum ve - ni - e.

Translation
Have mercy on those who suffer, Fount of Mercy.
You were merciful enough to bear the Prince of Glory;
honor of our race, ark of the new covenant, and dawn of grace:
surely if you wish, O kind Lady,
you can grant us peace and pardon.

Words: Latin, 13th c.; tran. and tr. Susan Hellauer © Susan Hellauer. All rights reserved. Used by permission.
Music: *Dublin Troper*, Irish, ca. 1390.

North Africa's mothers gave rise

1 North Af - ri - ca's mo - thers gave rise to the faith like
2 Dame Ju - li - an vis - ioned our cour - te - ous Lord; both
3 Oh, Je - sus, the guest, made his friends' hearts to turn— God's

Mon - i - ca, wo - man of wor - ship and prayer, her de - vo - tion con - vert - ed a
mo - ther and fa - ther to those who be - lieve. True love was the mean - ing, the
grace is a gift, not a work to be earned— 'twer Ma - ry and Mar - tha, dear

hus - band, two sons, and bless - ed is she, is she who be - lieves.
vis - ion to her, and bless - ed is she, is she who re - ceives.
friends of our Christ and bless - ed are they, are they who yearn.

O Monica, blest mother

1 O Mon - i - ca, blest mo - ther, a well of ho - ly tears; for
2 But Je - sus, Word In - car - nate re - vealed to him the truth; Aug -
3 Re - turned to his own home-land, as - sumed he Hip-po's see; staunch
4 Aug - us - tine, faith - ful bi - shop, con - fes - sor to the end, in -

thy dear son, Au - gus - tine, you shed for man - y years. That
gus - tine, thus con - vert - ed, for - sook his way - ward youth. Re -
cham - pion of the faith, he fought each her - e - sy. He
flame our hearts with pas - sion for Je - sus, Lord and friend. Au -

he might learn the faith that the Lord's a - pos - tles taught, but
nounc - ing Sa - tan's cun - ning, pre - vailed he in that hour; and
taught the church is ho - ly, though sin - ners do a - bound; that
gus - tine, ho - ly doc - tor, thou son of Af - ric's sod, help

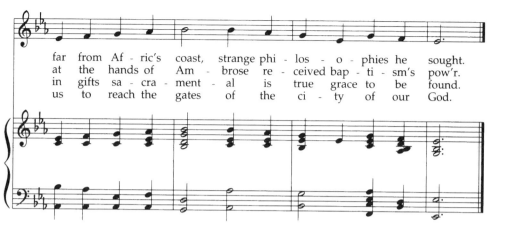

far from Af - ric's coast, strange phi - los - o - phies he sought.
at the hands of Am - brose re - ceived bap - ti - sm's pow'r.
in gifts sa - cra - ment - al is true grace to be found.
us to reach the gates of the ci - ty of our God.

Salamu Maria 11

1 Sa - la - mu Ma - ri - a, ee ma - ma,
2 U - me - ja - a nee - ma, ee ma - ma.

Sa - la - mu, sa - la - mu Ma - ri - a, Ma - ri - a; ri - a.

Translation

1 Hail Mary, O Mother,
  hail, hail Mary, Mary;

2 Full of grace, O Mother,
  hail, hail Mary.

Words: African folk hymn
Music: African melody

Litany for Sisters of the Christ

Refrain

Be your names re - mem - bered in the heart of God.

Be your names re - mem - bered in the heart of God.

Fine

Verses

1 Sis - ters of   the Christ,   you   who nursed the   truth,
2 Wo - men at   the birth,   wo - men   at   the   death,
3 You who stood the fire,   sis - ters drowned and hung,
4 You who taught the Word,   preached in   for - eign tongues,
5 You who lived the creeds,   you   who kept   the   hearth,
6 You who cher - ish life,   strug - gle on   for   peace,

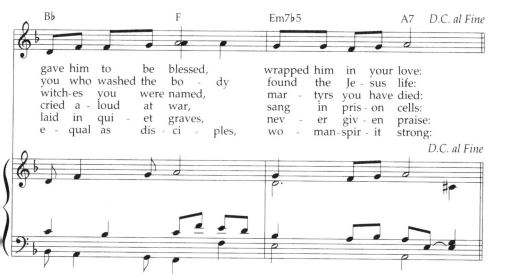

gave him to be blessed, wrapped him in your love:
you who washed the bo - dy found the Je - sus life:
witch - es you were named, mar - tyrs you have died:
cried a - loud at war, sang in pris - on cells:
laid in qui - et graves, nev - er giv - en praise:
e - qual as dis - ci - ples, wo - man - spir - it strong:

D.C. al Fine

Apostle of the Word

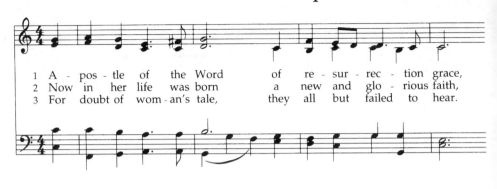

1 A - pos - tle of the Word of re - sur - rec - tion grace,
2 Now in her life was born a new and glo - rious faith,
3 For doubt of wom - an's tale, they all but failed to hear.

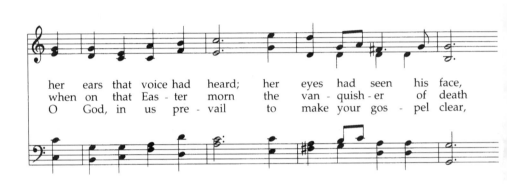

her ears that voice had heard; her eyes had seen his face,
when on that Eas - ter morn the van - quish - er of death
O God, in us pre - vail to make your gos - pel clear,

whose ris - en power with - in her heart bade grief de - part one shin - ing hour.
but spoke her name and found in her a mes - sen - ger with heart a - flame.
that nev - er may our hearts re - fuse, but ev - er choose your liv - ing way.

Words: Rosemary Anne Benwell, SSJD © The Sisterhood of St. John the Divine. All rights reserved. Used by permission.
Music: *Gopsal*, George Frideric Handel (1685-1759).

Delivered from shame

1 De - li - vered from shame, the wo - man came, with
2 His time had not come his life to be poured in
3 So sweet was the air with love ev - 'ry - where, the
4 A - lone was the night, the on - look-ers cried, "For

kneel - ing de - vo - tion sub - lime, to the feet of her Lord, and with
like - ness with gra - ti - tude shared. She wept at his feet, and
fra - grance of per - fume most rare. She knelt and she wept, sang her
shame!" for the waste of the nard. But her Je - sus, their Lord, whom she

tears a - dored her soon to be ri - sen Lord.
with her hair wiped tears from her eyes that o'er - flowed.
song of praise, a - ro - ma of love for her King.
loved, a - dored, with fra - grance sub - lime was ar - rayed.

5 The time was soon near his life to be spent, expensive a price for us all.
For the true Son of God would pour out his life in love for the world he adored.

6 The woman who wept, the one who received, were plan of divine nature bound.
Wrapped in fragrance of cost, spent in sorrow, loss, he rises, the fragrance of love.

And the women dancing

And the wo - men danc - ing with their tim - brels

fol - lowed Mir - iam as she sang her song.

Sing a song to the one whom we've ex - alt - ed,

Mir - iam and the wo - men danced and danced the whole night

To Final Refrain after Verse 3

long. _____

Verses

1 And
2 When
3

Mir-iam was a weav-er of u - nique va - ri - e - ty, the
Mir-iam stood up - on the shores and gazed a - cross the sea, the
Mi - ri - am the pro - phet took her tim - brel in her hand and

tap - es - try she wove was one which sang our his - to - ry, with
won-der of this mir - a - cle she soon came to be - lieve. Who-
all the wo - men fol - lowed her ___ just as she had planned. And

ev - ery strand and ev - ery thread she craft - ed her de - light, a
ev - er thought the sea would part ___ with an out - stretched hand, and
Mir-iam raised her voice in song, she sang with praise and might: "We've

wo - man touched with spi - rit, she dan - ces toward the
we would pass to free - dom and march to the prom - ised
just lived through a mir - a - cle, we're going to dance to -

Final Refrain (after Verse 3 and Refrain)

Sing a song to the one whom we've ex - al - ted,

Sing a song to the one whom we've ex - al - ted,

Mir - iam and the wo - men danced and danced the whole night

Mir - iam and the wo - men danced and danced the whole night

long. _____

long. _____

1 With Mir - iam we will dance and ce - le - brate the day
2 With Ma - ry we will wait when ev - en hope seems dead
3 With Con - stance we will stand for what we know is right
4 Made whole, the hu - man race may an - swer to God's call

when sul - len seas were swept a - part to show the way.
when o - thers rush down roads they say we may not tread.
in an - swer to God's just de - mand and search - ing sight,
in dance and si - lence, truth and grace, em - brac - ing all.

The danc - ers lend us grace to turn from seas of fear
And wait - ing, strong and still through all our grief and pain
con - front - ing each a - buse that stran - gles li - ber - ty,
This jour - ney ne - ver ends, God's pro - mise calls us on,

to - wards the un - known wil - der - ness for God is there.
we hear the whis - per of God's will we hear our name.
God help us simp - ly state the truth that sets us free.
un - til our sis - ters, bro - thers, friends may join the song.

Words: Janet Wootton © 1998 Stainer and Bell Ltd. (admin. Hope Publishing Company, Carol Stream, IL 60188). All
         rights reserved. Used by permission.
Music: *Leoni*, Hebrew melody; harm. *Hymns Ancient and Modern*, 1875, alt.
You must contact Hope Publishing Company to reproduce these words.

Arise, Devorah

Refrain

A - rise, a - rise, De - vo - rah, a - rise, a - rise and sing a song. A - rise, a - rise, De - vo - rah.

After Verse 2, To Bridge

Fine

U - ri, u - ri, da - b'ri shir.

1 De-
2 De-
3 De-

Verses

vo-rah, the pro-phet, was a judge in Is - ra - el.
vo-rah, the pro-phet, was cou - ra - geous, strong and wise.
vo-rah, the pro-phet, a wo - man of fire her torch in hand.

She sat be - neath her palm tree on the hill, _____
Her peo-ple lived in peace for for - ty years. _____
She led the Is - rael - ites to vic - to - ry. _____

and peo - ple came from e - ve - ry - where just to hear
The twelve tribes lived to - geth - er as one, for the first
Ba - rak said "D'vo - rah, I can-not fight un-less you

__ her judge-ments, hon - est and fair.
__ time since the world had be - gun. De - vo-rah, the pro - phet, De - vo-
__ are stand-ing right by my side."

- rah, a mo - ther in Is - ra - el. __ A - rise, a -

D.S.

D.S.

"Uri, uri, dab'ri shir" means "Arise and sing a song" in Hebrew.

Rejoice for women brave

18

1 Re - joice for wo - men brave, who laughed and cried and sang, who
2 Re - joice for Sa - rah's mirth; she lis - tened laugh-ing - ly. In
3 Re - joice for Han-nah, bold; she loud - ly made her plea. Then
4 Your gra-cious love di - vine, like Mir - iam we pro - claim. May

lis - tened to an - gels, be - lieved their God, from them sal - va - tion sprang.
joy she brought forth a new na - tion, say - ing all will laugh with me.
God heard her prayers and she, ex - ul - tant, sang of vic - to - ry.
we now sing praise and with Ma - ry mag - ni - fy your ho - ly name.

Refrain

Lift up your heart, lift up your voice, re - joice, a - gain I

say re-joice, re - joice a - gain, I say re - joice.

Words: Lisa Neufeld Thomas © 2001 Lisa Neufeld Thomas. All rights reserved. Used by permission.
Music: *Mayfair*, Frances McCollin (1892-1960).

O wind that blows

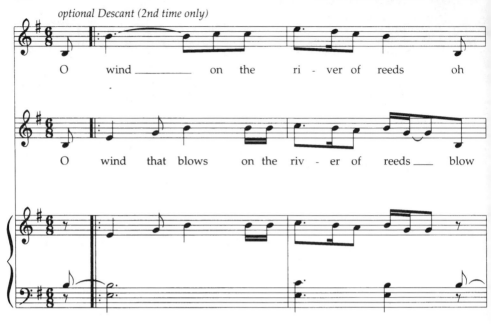

optional Descant (2nd time only)

O wind _____ on the ri - ver of reeds oh

O wind that blows on the riv - er of reeds _____ blow

wind _____ mel - o - dies, oh wind _____

Mo - she his mo - ther's sweet mel - o - dies. Rock him in your

keep him safe and warm. Oh warm.

wa-ter-y womb and keep him safe and warm. Oh warm.

There was Jesus by the water

1 There was Je - sus by the wa - ter speak-ing to the press-ing crowd, when, be - hold, there came a ru - ler from the syn - a - gogue, who bowed, say - ing
2 As the Sa - vior healed an - oth - er, news was brought that she was dead. "Do not trou - ble Je - sus fur - ther." Je - sus heard the news and said, "I will
3 Je - sus went back with the ru - ler where they heard the mourn-ers weep. Je - sus said un - to the wail - ers, "Why this tu - mult she's a - sleep. I will
4 Je - sus touched the lit - tle daugh - ter say - ing "Lit - tle girl a - rise!" And she rose to see her fa - ther and her mo - ther's stunned sur - prise. They then

"Come and heal my daugh - ter, lay your heal - ing hands up -
come and see your daugh - ter, I will lay my hands up -
go un - to his daugh - ter, and will lay my hands up -
held their lit - tle daugh - ter and they laid their hands up -

on her, heal her, Lord, that she may live."
on her, do not fear, she yet may live."
on her, do not laugh, on - ly be - lieve."
on her, trust - ing how he made her live.

Words: Gracia Grindal © Selah Publishing Company, 58 Pearl Street, P.O. Box 3037, Kingston, NY 12402.
         www.selahpub.com. All rights reserved. Used by permission.
Music: *Talitha cumi*, Rusty Edwards © 1983 Hope Publishing Company, Carol Stream, IL 60188. All rights reserved.
         Used by permission.
You must contact Selah Publishing Company to reproduce these words, and Hope Publishing Company to reproduce this music.

21
God of the women

1 God of the wo - men who an - swered your call,
2 God of the wo - men who walked Je - sus' way,
3 God of the wo - men long put to the test,
4 God of the wo - men who ran from the tomb,
5 O God of Phoe - be and min - is - ters all,

trust - ing your prom - ise, giv - ing their all,
giv - ing their re - sour - ces, learn - ing to pray,
left out of sto - ries, for - got - ten, op - pressed,
prayed with the o - thers in that up - per room,
may we be joy - ful in answer-ing your call.

wo - men like Sar - ah and Han - nah and Ruth _____
Ma - ry, Jo - an - na, Sus - an - na, and more _____
qui - et - ly ask - ing: "Who smiled at my birth?" _____
then felt your Spi - rit on Pen - te - cost Day _____
give us the strength of your Spi - rit so near _____

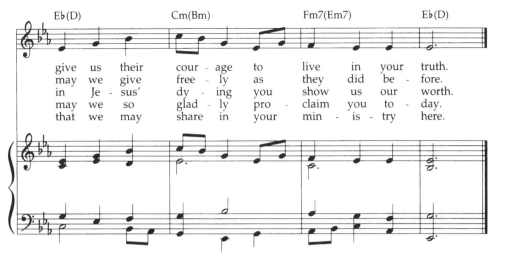

Eb(D)　　　　　Cm(Bm)　　　　Fm7(Em7)　　　Eb(D)

give	us	their	cour - age	to	live	in	your	truth.
may	we	give	free - ly	as	they	did	be -	fore.
in	Je -	sus'	dy - ing	you	show	us	our	worth.
may	we	so	glad - ly	pro -	claim	you	to -	day.
that	we	may	share	in	your	min - is - try	here.

Capo 1, play D. Keyboard and guitar should not sound together.

In life's busy moments　　　　　　　　　　　22

1	In	life's	bu - sy	mo - ments	we	cir - cle	in	haste,
2	While	Ma - ry	her	sis - ter	sat	list' - ning	in	awe,
3		Pres - ent	in	con - flict	en -	rich - ing	our	souls,
4	Al - le - lu - ia,	he	comes ___	in	glo - rious	ar - ray;

like	Mar - tha	so	wor - ried	when	Je - sus	she	faced.
the	Lord	spoke	of	God's	love	em - brac - ing	us	all.
with	Ma - ry	and	Mar - tha	he	loves	and	con - soles.
we	pause	in	dai - ly	life	to	pon - der	and	pray.

Refrain

He comes to vis - it, he comes to share; we learn to lis - ten, we learn to care.

May be sung in Canon
* Word accentuation for verse 4: 2 + 2 + 2

A father came to Jesus

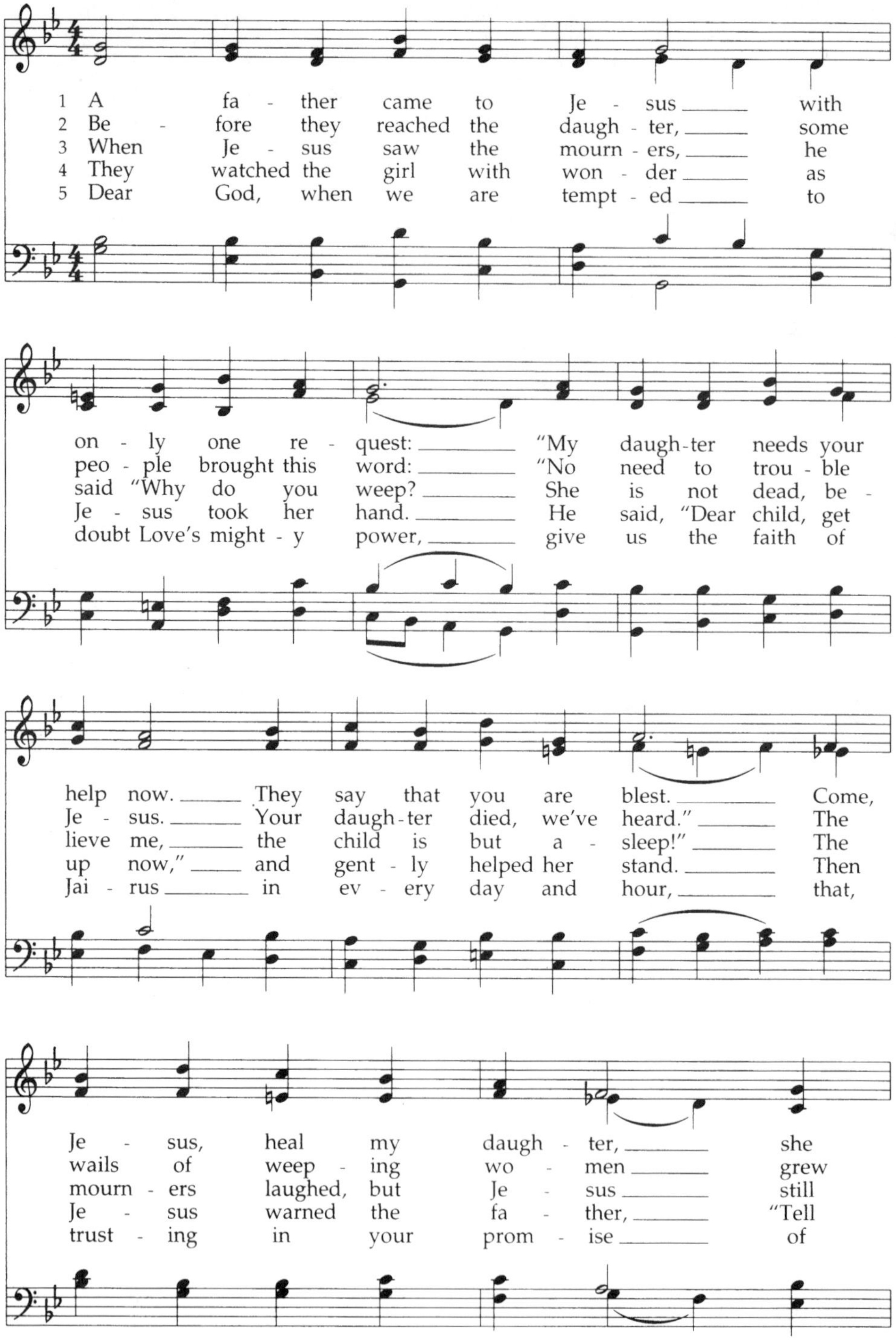

lies so close to death._____ Come, lay your hands up -
loud as they drew near,_____ but Je - sus told the
took his friends in - side._____ The faith - ful par - ents
no one that you meet,"_____ and asked the grate - ful
ev - er last - ing care,_____ we all may lay be -

on her_____ while she has life and breath."
fa - ther,_____ "Be - lieve and do not fear."
fol - lowed _____ to see what would be - tide.
mo - ther _____ to bring her food to eat.
fore you_____ our deep - est needs in prayer.

1 When, like the woman at the well, I
2 Christ knew my heart, my way - ward ways, yet
3 I learned I could for - ev - er live and
4 Each day I lift my cup a - bove and
5 Since now I am in grace im - mersed, set

lived with bro - ken dreams,____ Christ came to me, good
gave me hope, not fear.____ The God I once thought
wor - ship God a - right,____ could trust the power the
once a - gain re - ceive____ the liv - ing wa - ter
free, for - giv - en, whole,____ I share with those who

Fine

news to tell, of ev - er liv - ing streams.____
far a - way, I could ap - proach, draw near.____
Spi - rit gives to guide me in truth's light.____
of God's love, re - vealed for my be - lief.____
are a - thirst the well - springs of my soul.____

Fine

Unison or harmony

1 Je - sus de - scribes a force - ful wo - man, a wid - ow who re -
2 And day by day she spoke for jus - tice, and word by word in -
3 Now we, ob - serv - ing, are in - vit - ed to re - col - lect what

fused to bend be - fore a judge, a man of pow - er,
jus - tice waned un - til im - pas - sive will re - lent - ed,
faith can gain when faith - ful peo - ple are un - daunt - ed

whose judg - ments worked to no good end: she knew that she had
and her im - pas - sioned faith re - mained: be - liev - ing God would
and hope, in con - flict, is sus - tained: as we, like she, wield

pow - er, too, and trust - ed in the strength she knew.
make a way, she found the grace that faith con - veys.
stub - born trust, God comes to move the world through us.

Music: *Wer nur den lieben Gott*, Georg Neumark (1621-1681).

Women of faith

1. Wo - men of faith, lov - ing and kind,
2. Wea - pon of truth, Ra - hab o - beyed.
3. Ma - ry per - ceived, Ma - ry be - lieved.
4. Sa - vior of all, now we re - call,

gift from the Fa - ther, bold and free. Sent to the need - y,
Led by the Spi - rit, o - pened wide. Put out the red cord,
Je - sus a - live, in love re - vealed. Sent to the hearts of
"Fear not!" with fa - vor, come to us. Lord, we be - lieve you,

wor - ship the ma - jes - ty,
sign to de - li - ver,   Al - le - lu - ia!   A - men.   *Optional Ending*
those who be - lieved her.   *(After final verse)*
Lord, we re - ceive you.

I will kindle my fire

I will kin-dle my fire in the morn of the day, in the pres-ence of ho-ly an - gels. With-out mal - ice or jeal - ous-y, en - vy or fear, with-out ter - ror of an - y-one un - der the sun, but the Ho - ly Be-lov - ed to shield me.

O Ho - ly one, kin - dle thou here in my heart, a flame of pure love to my neigh - bor, to my foe, to my friend, to my kin - dred all, to the brave, to the knave, to the thrall. O child of the love-li-est Ma - ry, from the low - li-est thing, to the Ho - ly Name, the be - lov - ed of all.

Knave: unprincipled, crafty person
Thrall: one who is in bondage

Words: *Carmina Gadelica*, alt.
Music: Mary Truly Ermey © 1998 St. Hildegard's Community. All rights reserved. Used by permission.

Our God, we thank thee for the night

1 Our God, we thank thee for the night, and for the pleas-ant
2 Help us, to do the things we should, to be to oth - ers

morn - ing light, for rest and food and lov - ing care, and
kind and good, may all we do in work or play be

For canon only

all that makes the day so fair. (the day so fair.)
done with love and rest this day. (and rest this day.)

This hymn may be sung unaccompanied as a four-part canon at a distance of one measure.

Words: Rebecca J. Weston, 1885.
Music: *The Eighth Tune*, Thomas Tallis (1505?-1585).

Guide us waking

Guide us wa-king guard us sleep-ing that a - wake we watch with Christ,

and a - sleep we may rest in peace.

This first page should be repeated several times before the next voice enters on the next page. Then the parts numbered 1 and 2 sing through once or twice and part 3 comes in, etc. There is no end to the tune, and you may continue as long as forever, or bring the parts out in reverse order (8-7-6 etc.) for a tidier finish. The fermata is observed only for the final repetition.

30

Still, still with thee

Words: Harriet Beecher Stowe (1812-1896).
Music: *Consolation*, Felix Mendelssohn (1809-1847).

When candles are lighted

1. When can - dles are light - ed on Can - dle - mas Day
2. The kings have de - part - ed, the shep - herds have gone,
3. They go to the tem - ple, o - bey - ing the law,

the dark is be - hind us, and Spring's on the way.
the child and his par - ents are left on their own.
and of - fer two pi - geons, the gift of the poor.

A glo - ry dawns in ev - ery dark place,

the light of Christ, the full - ness of grace.

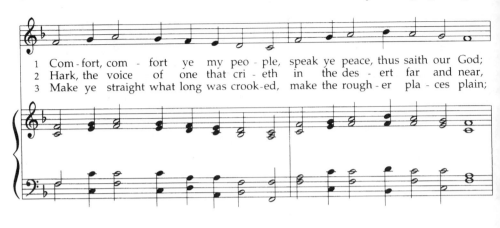

1 Com-fort, com - fort ye my peo - ple, speak ye peace, thus saith our God;
2 Hark, the voice of one that cri - eth in the des - ert far and near,
3 Make ye straight what long was crook-ed, make the rough - er pla - ces plain;

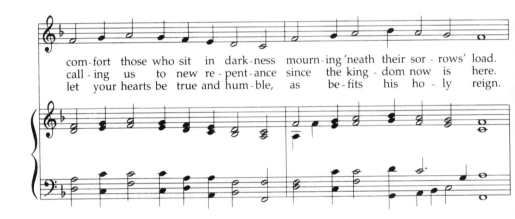

com-fort those who sit in dark-ness mourn-ing 'neath their sor - rows' load.
call - ing us to new re - pent-ance since the king - dom now is here.
let your hearts be true and hum-ble, as be - fits his ho - ly reign.

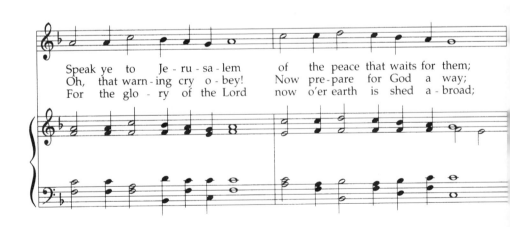

Speak ye to Je - ru - sa - lem of the peace that waits for them;
Oh, that warn - ing cry o - bey! Now pre - pare for God a way;
For the glo - ry of the Lord now o'er earth is shed a - broad;

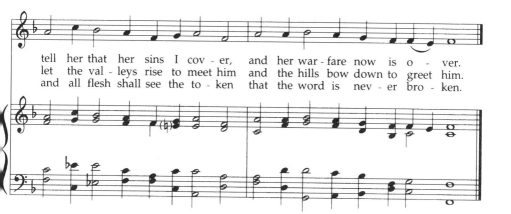

tell her that her sins I cov - er, and her war - fare now is o - ver.
let the val - leys rise to meet him and the hills bow down to greet him.
and all flesh shall see the to - ken that the word is nev - er bro - ken.

Words: Johannes Olearius (1611-1684); tr. Catherine Winkworth (1827-1878), alt.
Music: *Psalm 42*, melody Claude Goudimel (1514-1572).

The grain is ripe

1 The grain is ripe: the har - vest comes!
2 The right - eous God gives this ___ and more:
3 The work of peace is all ___ for all,

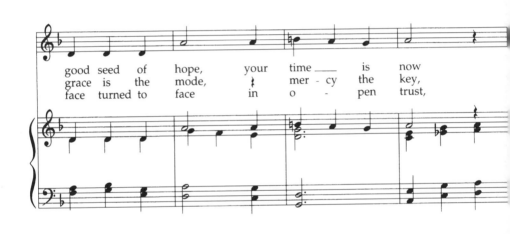

good seed of hope, your time ___ is now
grace is the mode, mer - cy the key,
face turned to face in o - pen trust,

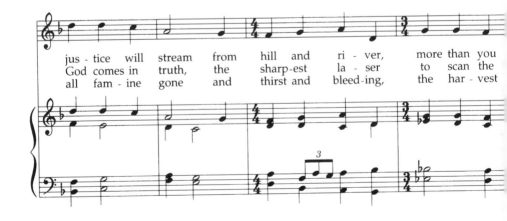

jus - tice will stream from hill and ri - ver, more than you
God comes in truth, the sharp-est la - ser to scan the
all fam - ine gone and thirst and bleed-ing, the har - vest

dream __ and run - - - ning o - ver.
earth, __ to take _____ our mea - sure.
comes __ from love's _____ good seed - ing.

People, look East

1 Peo - ple, look East. The time is near of the
2 Fur - rows, be glad. Though earth is bare, one more
3 Birds, though you long have ceased to build, guard the
4 Stars, keep the watch. When night is dim one more
5 An - gels, an - nounce with shouts of mirth Christ who

crown - ing of the year. Make your house fair as you are
seed is plant - ed there: give up your strength the seed to
nest that must be filled. E - ven the hour when wings are
light the bowl shall brim, shin - ing be - yond the frost - y
brings new life to earth. Set ev - ery peak and val - ley

a - ble, trim the hearth and set the ta - ble.
nour - ish, that in course the flow'r may flour - ish.
fro - zen God for fledg - ing time has cho - sen. Peo - ple, look
weath - er, bright as sun and moon to - geth - er.
hum - ming with the word, the Lord is com - ing.

East and sing to-day: Love the guest is on the way.

1 Star - Child, earth - Child, go - be - tween of God,
2 Street child, beat child, no place left to go,
3 Grown child, old child, mem - ory full of years,
4 Spared child, spoiled child, hav - ing, want - ing more,
5 Hope - for peace Child, God's stu - pen - dous sign,

love Child, Christ Child, hea - ven's light - ning rod,
hurt child, used child no one wants to know,
sad child, lost child, sto - ry told in tears,
wise child, faith child, know-ing joy in store,
down - to earth Child, Star of stars that shine,

Refrain

This year, this year, let the day ar - rive, when

Christ-mas comes for ev-ery-one, ev-ery-one a - live!

O mundi domina 36

O __ mun-di do - mi - na, re - gi-o ex se - mi - ne __ or - ta:

ex tu - o jam Chris-tus pro - ces - sit al - vo, _____

tam-quam spon-sus __ de __ tha - la - mo; hic ia - cet in

prae-se - pi - o, _____ qui et si - de - ra re - git.

Translation:
O mistress of the world, descended from royal seed:
from your womb Christ has come forth,
like the bridegroom from the bridal bed;
he lies in the crib, who rules the stars.

Mary borned a baby

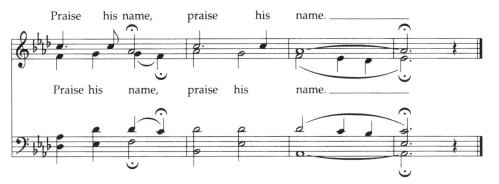

Praise his name, praise his name.

Praise his name, praise his name.

Words: Traditional
Music: Negro Spiritual; arr. Noah Francis Ryder (1914-1964).

1 Once in roy-al Da-vid's ci-ty stood a low-ly cat-tle shed, where a mo-ther laid her ba-by in a man-ger for his bed: Ma-ry was that mo-ther mild, Je-sus Christ her lit-tle child.

2 He came down to earth from hea-ven, who is God and Lord of all, and his shel-ter was a sta-ble, and his cra-dle was a stall; with the poor, and mean, and low-ly, lived on earth our Sa-viour ho-ly.

3 And, thro' all his won-drous child-hood, he would hon-or and o-bey, love, and watch the low-ly maid-en in whose gen-tle arms he lay; Chris-tian chil-dren all must be mild, o-be-dient, good as he.

4 For he is our child-hood's pat-tern; day by day like us he grew; he was lit-tle, weak, and help-less, tears and smiles like us he knew; and he feel-eth for our sad-ness, and he shar-eth in our glad-ness.

5 And our eyes at last shall see him, through his own re-deem-ing love; for that child so dear and gen-tle is our Lord in heav'n a-bove; and he leads his child-ren on to the place where he is gone.

Words: Cecil Frances Alexander (1818-1895) © G. Schirmer, Inc., 257 Park Avenue South, NY, NY 10010.
         All rights reserved. Used by permission.
Music: *Irby*, Henry J. Gauntlett (1805-1876).

6   Not in that poor lowly stable,
        With the Oxen standing by,
    We shall see him; but in heaven,
        Set at God's right hand on high;
    When like stars his children crowned,
    All in white shall wait around.

Eternity touched hands with time   39

1 E - ter - ni - ty touched hands with time when Ma - ry
2 The an - gels shared in earth's de - light, a star be -
3 Time still can touch e - ter - ni - ty, when we reach

said, "God's will be done," and com - mon - place be -
came the ma - gi's sign, and shep - herds met, on
out to God in prayer; re - joice that Christ will

came sub - lime when that young wo - man bore a son.
Christ-mas night, a child, both hu - man and di - vine.
ev - er be re - born in hearts that want him there!

Words: Rae E. Whitney © Selah Publishing Company, Inc., 58 Pearl Street, P.O. Box 3037, Kingston, NY 12401.
         www.selahpub.com. All rights reserved. Used by permission.
Music: *Conditor alme siderum*, plainsong, Mode 4; acc. Bruce Neswick © 2002 Bruce Neswick. All rights reserved.
         Used by permission.
You must contact Selah Publishing to reproduce these words.

O Lord God

O _____ Lord _____ God, the wo - man who had

Drone (unison)

ee _____

fall - en _____ in - to man - y _____ sins, _____

man - y _____ sins, _____

hav-ing per-ceived thy di - vin - i -

ee _____

ty, re-ceived the rank of oint - ment - bear - er, _____

of - fer-ing thee spi - ces be - fore _____

I will wipe _____ them with my tres - ses,

tres - ses,

from thy hand - maid - en, O thou _____ of

ee _____

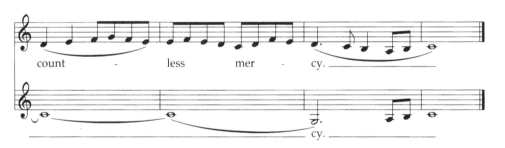

count - less mer - cy. _____

cy. _____

O Lord, how the fallen woman wept

1 O Lord, how the fal-len wo-man wept when she be-held your
2 "O woe," hear her cry, "O woe is me for I am lost in
3 "To you, who draws o-ceans to the clouds, I give the foun-tain
4 "Now see: I shall kiss your sa-cred feet, and I shall dry them
5 "O who, then, can com-pre-hend my sins? And who can grasp your

ho - li - ness,   and with great sor - row brought myrrh and
wil - der - ness!   My love of sin brought me deep - est
of my tears!   You've shown the joys ___ of heav'n to
with my hair;   those feet whose tread ___ in E - den's
judge-ments deep? Thou, blest Re - deem-er of count - less

spice,   an - noint-ing you for par - a - dise.
night,   my way is dark; there is ___ no light.
me;   in mer - cy hear my ag - o - ny.
groves caused Eve to hide her face ___ in dread.
souls: re - mem-ber me, re - mem - ber me."

Words: Kassia the Nun (ca. 805); adapt. CCW Sparks © 2000 Ralamar Sparks Enterprises; vers. Esta Cassway
© 2001 Ralamar Sparks Enterprises. All rights reserved. Used by permission.
Music: Robert A.M. Ross © 2001 Ralamar Sparks Enterprises. All rights reserved. Used by permission.

Would you share Christ's passion?   42

1 Would you share Christ's pas - sion? Take your cross and fol - low;
2 Would you know Christ's mean - ing, daz - zling in its ra - diance?
3 Would you join Christ's tri - umph, o - ver death vic - to - rious,

climb Gol - ga - tha's hill. Taste the cup of sor - row, wine and gall com-
Lie down in the fire. Brave the flames of Wis - dom, sear - ing with their
ris - ing from the grave? Pain and grief are fore - courts of the heav'n - ly

min - gled: drink its bit - ter fill. Bear the scourge of doubt and fear.
myst - 'ry, fierce with Love's de - sire. Cast the dark - ened glass a - way:
ci - ty, bought with blood he gave. Suf - f'ring marks the nar - row gate.

Though a jeer - ing crowd de - ride you, he will walk be - side you.
O - pen to a bril - liant burn - ing. Seek and find true learn - ing.
Yet, though tri - als throng to greet you, none shall now de - feat you!

Words: Mary Louise Bringle © 2002 GIA Publications, Inc. All rights reserved. Used by permission.
Music: *Jesu, meine Freude*, Johann Crüger (1598-1662), alt.
You must contact GIA Publications to reproduce these words.

At the foot of the cross

1 At the foot of the cross
2 Bles-sed Ma-ry, his mother
3 Now with love in their hearts
4 When it was finished,
5 At the foot of the cross

Ma - ry sat weep - ing and gaz - ing with love at her
bore him and rocked him and bathed him with love for her
Ma - ry and John sat to - geth - er and poured out their
Je - sus was laid in a tomb wrapped in grave clothes of
we sit with Ma - ry and wor - ship with love in our

Lord. He hung there bleed - ing and
son. Saw him in child - hood and
grief. "Look, John, your moth - er" and
death. Three long nights af - ter,
hearts. For he has ri - sen and

suf - fering and dy - ing. She could not help him.
grow - ing to man - hood. She could not help him.
"Ma - ry, your son, John." She could not help him.
he left the grave clothes. She did not help him.
lives with his Fa - ther. We on - ly love him.

Final Ending

She could not car - ry him home. _____
She could not car - ry him home. _____
She could not car - ry him home. _____
She did not car - ry him home. _____
He lives to car - ry us home. _____

Mary and Martha's just gone 'long

1 Ma - ry and - a Mar - tha's just gone 'long, Ma - ry and - a Mar - tha's
2 prea-cher and the eld - er's just gone 'long, the prea-cher and the eld - er's
3 My fa - ther and moth-er's just gone 'long, my fa - ther and moth-er's

just gone 'long, Ma - ry and - a Mar - tha's just gone 'long to
just gone 'long, the prea-cher and the el - der's just gone 'long to
just gone 'long, my fa - ther and moth-er's just gone 'long to

ring those charm-ing bells; cry-ing, free grace and dy-ing love, free grace and

dy-ing love, free grace and dy-ing love, to ring those charm-ing bells.

Oh, 'way o - ver Jor - dan, Lord, 'way o - ver Jor - dan, Lord,

'way o - ver Jor - dan, Lord, to ring those charm-ing bells. (2) The

Words: Traditional
Music: Negro Spiritual; ed. R. Nathaniel Dett (1882-1943) © CPP/Belwin Inc. (admin. Warner Brothers Publications,
Inc.). All rights reserved. Used by permission.

That Easter morn

Refrain

Al - le - lu - ia!___ Al - le - lu - ia! Al - le - lu - ia!

1 That Eas - ter morn, at break of day, a faith - ful wo - man
2 When Ma - ry's heart was filled with gloom as she stood weep - ing
3 "Why do you weep?" his ques - tion came? "Whose is the bo - dy
4 No long - er weep - ing, an - guish-bent, but with re - joic - ing

went her way to seek the tomb where Je - sus lay. Al-le-lu - ia!
near the tomb, a strang-er spoke, she knew not whom. Al-le-lu - ia!
you would claim?" And then, at last, he spoke her name. Al-le-lu - ia!
Ma - ry went, by Christ, the first a - pos - tle sent. Al-le-lu - ia!

Words: St. 1 Jean Tisserand (?-1494); tr. John Mason Neale (1818-1866), alt. ; Sts. 2, 3, 4, Delores Dufner, OSB
© 1994 Sisters of St. Benedict, St. Joseph, MN. All rights reserved. Used by permission.
Music: *O filii et filiae,* melody from *Airs sur les hymnes sacrez, odes et noëls,* 1623; acc. Carl Haywood © Carl Haywood.
All rights reserved. Used by permission.
You must contact Carl Haywood to reproduce this accompaniment.

1 Em - man - u - el! The an - gels' an - cient cho - rus
2 Em - man - u - el! He laid a - side his splen-dor,
3 Em - man - u - el! This Je - sus, meek and low - ly,
4 Em - man - u - el! Our God in us is dwell-ing,

to - day un - folds be - fore us, the fi - nal tri - umph starts.
and par - a - dise sur - ren - dered that we might be set free.
has made us sin - ners ho - ly, by his al - might-y blood.
our God, with - in us, tell - ing that he has come to save.

Em - man - u - el! With - in that name a trea - sure,
Em - man - u - el! He ris - es now vic - to - rious,
Em - man - u - el! For - give - ness has been spo - ken,
Em - man - u - el! The an - gels sing their sto - ry,

an - nounc-ing God's good plea-sure to dwell with-in our hearts.
to live for - ev - er glo - rious, and reign e - ter - nal - ly.
the king - dom now is o - pen, and we be - hold our God!
of Christ, our hope of glo - ry, the King is ris'n to - day!

O Mary, O Martha

47

Words: Traditional
Music: Negro Spiritual; arr. Horace Clarence Boyer © 1992 Horace Clarence Boyer. All rights reserved. Used by permission.

Words: Adapt. *Matthew* 28:1-7.
Music: Sulpitia Cesis (1619), acc. Robert A.M. Ross © 2001 Ralamar Sparks Enterprises. All rights reserved.
Used by permission.

Translation:
Mary Magdalene and the other Mary
went to the place of the sepulchre.

It is Jesus whom you seek.
He is not here;
he is risen as He said, and goes before you to Galilee.
There you will see Him.

There is a green hill far away 49

At break of day

1 At break of day three wo-men came to find where Christ was laid.
2 O Ma - ry, see your son a - gain, in re - sur - rec - tion joy.
3 Come ce - le - brate the death of death! Come share e - ter - nal life!

With myrrh pre - pared to a - noint his corpse, they wept and mourned the dead.
Shine, shine Je - ru - sa - lem, for Christ is risen in ma - jes - ty.
Come leap and praise the liv - ing God who o - pens par - a - dise!

But now the stone is rolled a - way, they wor - ship in full day,
Lift up your eyes, look round and see, re - joic - ing, strong and free,
For dawn is come all shin - ing bright, to show sal - va - tion's might

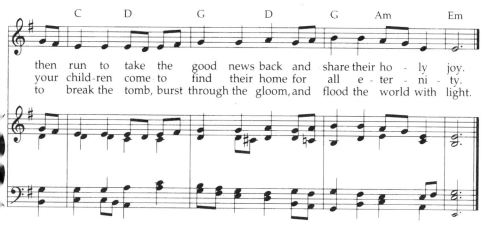

then run to take the good news back and share their holy joy.
your children come to find their home for all eternity.
to break the tomb, burst through the gloom, and flood the world with light.

Keyboard and guitar should not sound together.

Words: Janet Wootton © 1991 Stainer and Bell Ltd. (admin. Hope Publishing Company, Carol Stream, IL 60188). All rights reserved. Used by permission.
Music: *Kingsfold*, English melody; adapt. Ralph Vaughan Williams (1872-1958).
You must contact Hope Publishing Company to reproduce these words.

Loving Spirit   51

1 Loving Spirit, loving Spirit, you have chosen me to be;
2 Like a mother you enfold me, hold my life within your own,
3 Like a father you protect me, teach me the discerning eye,
4 Friend and lover in your closeness I am known and held and blessed,
5 Loving Spirit, loving Spirit, you have chosen me to be;

you have drawn me to your wonder, you have set your sign on me.
feed me with your very body, form me of your flesh and bone.
hoist me up upon your shoulder, let me see the world from high.
in your promise is my comfort, in your presence I may rest.
you have drawn me to your wonder, you have set your sign on me.

Words: Shirley Erena Murray © 1987 The Hymn Society (admin. Hope Publishing Company, Carol Stream, IL 60188). All rights reserved. Used by permission.
Music: *Omni die*, melody from *Gross Catolisch Gesangbuch*, 1631; harm. William Smith Rockstro (1823-1895).
You must contact Hope Publishing Company to reproduce these words.

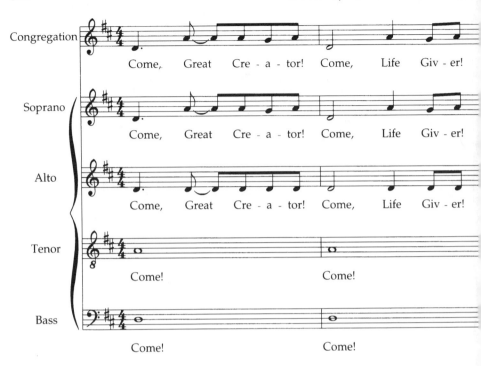

O-si-yo means hello and goodbye, welcome and peace.

    O = o
    si = see
    yo = o

Verses may be sung by a solo voice and the choir may sing the same accompaniment for all verses.

Spirit of God, unseen

53

Spi-rit of God, un-seen as the wind, gen-tle as is the dove:

teach us the truth and help us be-lieve, show us the Sa-viour's love! love!

1 You spoke to us long, long a-go, gave us the writ-ten word;
2 With-out your help we fail our Lord, we can-not live his way;

we read it still, need-ing its truth, through it God's voice is heard.
we need your power, we need your strength, fol - low-ing Christ each day.

Words: Margaret Old (1932-2002) © Scripture Union. Used by permission. All rights reserved.
Music: *Skye Boat Song*, Scottish traditional melody; arr. James Whitbourn © Oxford University Press. All rights reserved. Used by permission.
You must contact Oxford University Press to reproduce this arrangement.

O Holy Spirit

1 O Holy Spirit, flow - ing light,
2 O Holy Spirit, wis - dom's fire,
3 O Holy Spirit, heal - ing balm,
4 O Holy Spirit, heav'n - ly dove,
5 O Holy Spirit, par - a - clete,

of sun's gold sheen and mir - ror's bright:
of leap - ing flame and stee - ple's spire,
of scent - filled air and salv - ing calm:
reach through the lat - tice of your love,
make strong our hands and swift our feet,

re - flect in us your clear de - light.
up - lift our in - tel - lect's de - sire.
dis - till our tears to cry - stal psalm.
and train us toward the life a - bove,
to serve the Christ in all we meet.

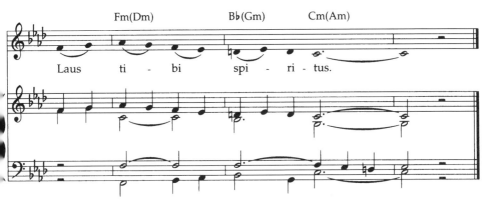

Laus ti - bi spi - ri - tus.

Capo 3, play Am.

Words: Mary Louise Bringle, after Hildegard of Bingen (1098-1179) © 2002 GIA Publications, Inc. All rights reserved. Used by permission.

Music: Mary Louise Bringle © 2002 GIA Publications, Inc.; arr. Barry Rose © 2001 Barry Rose. All rights reserved. Used by permission.

You must contact GIA Publications to reproduce this selection.

O Holy Spirit, root of life

Descant

3 stored. O ho - ly wis - dom, soar -

1 O Ho - ly Spi - rit, root of life cre - a - tor, cleans - er
2 (E) - ter - nal Vig - or, sav - ing one, you free us by your
3 (O) Ho - ly Wis - dom, soar - ing pow'r, en - com - pass us with

- ing Pow'r, car - ry us, en - cir - cling all, a -

of all things, a - noint our wounds, a - wak - en us with lus - trous
liv - ing Word, be - com - ing flesh to wear our pain, and all cre -
wings un - furled, and car - ry us, en - cir - cling all, a - bove, be -

God of flowing light

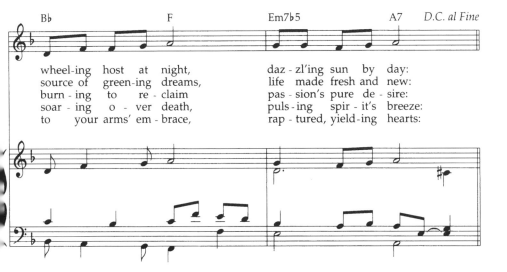

wheel-ing host at night,   daz - zl'ing sun by day:
source of green-ing dreams,   life made fresh and new:
burn - ing to re - claim   pas - sion's pure de - sire:
soar - ing o - ver death,   puls - ing spir - it's breeze:
to your arms' em - brace,   rap - tured, yield-ing hearts:

Words: Mary Louise Bringle © 2002 GIA Publications, Inc. All rights reserved. Used by permission.
Music: CCW Sparks; arr. Robert A.M. Ross © 2000 Ralamar Sparks Enterprises. All rights reserved. Used by permission.

No longer settled

1 No long - er set - tled or sure of our ways we
2 Claim - ing our pas - sion, em - brac - ing our rage
3 Voic - es long si - lenced and mem - 'ries de - nied

leave our - selves o - pen, in mo - ments of grace, to
strength-ens our love to re - fash - ion this age, un -
call out for heal - ing, for jus - tice and pride. Our

fresh ways of see - ing— scales fall from our eyes and
leash - es the pow - er to chal - lenge our lies and
hearts hear the an - guish of each sa - cred cry and

in our new vis - ions, the Spi - rit shall rise.
in right-eous an - ger, the Spi - rit shall rise.
in our com - pas - sion, the Spi - rit shall rise.

Spirit of God

1 Spi - rit of God, you moved o - ver the wa - ters
2 Spi - rit of God, by the pro - phets you sought us,
3 Spi - rit of God, like a dove you once rest - ed,
4 Spi - rit of God, like a might - y wind blow - ing:
5 Help us to see you, still call - ing and car - ing,

whisp-'ring God's love to the whole of cre - a - tion.
cal - ling us back from our pride - filled be - ha - vior.
show - ing God's joy on the day Christ was bap - tized.
sud - den - ly Chris - tians stopped hid - ing and fear - ing.
help us to know you a - mong us, cre - at - ing.

You breathe your life in - to God's sons and daugh - ters,
Through cho - sen lead - ers you reached us and taught us;
You sent Christ out to the hills to be test - ed,
You gave them cour - age and love o - ver - flow - ing,
Spi - rit of God, give us cour - age and dar - ing—

giv - ing us tal - ents and your in - spi - ra - tion.
by your own gift we were giv - en our Sav - ior.
through you, he called us to see God with new eyes.
so they pro - claimed you to all in their hear - ing.
to share God's love with a world that is wait - ing.

Words: Carolyn Winfrey Gillette © 1999 Carolyn Winfrey Gillette, from *Gifts of Love: New Hymns for Today's Worship*
(Geneva Press, 2000). All rights reserved. Used by permission.
Music: *O quanta qualia*, melody from *Antiphoner*, 1681.

Breath of God

59

1 Breath of God, life - bear - ing wind, wak - ing
2 Breath of God, word - bear - ing wind, truth—re -
3 Breath of God, fire - bear - ing wind, source of
4 Breath of God, song - bear - ing wind, stir - ring

mat - ter in - to birth, plant-ing prom - ise, prompt-ing
veal - er, pro - phet's speech, guide to vis - tas of the
pow - er, love, and light, melt - ing fears and join - ing
won - der to re - joice, yearn-ing's ech - o, gra - ce's

hope: with your life re - new the earth.
mind: let your word ex - cite and teach.
tongues: with your fire our hearts ig - nite.
dance: let your song give our prayers voice.

Come and seek the ways of Wisdom

Descant

3 O _____ vir - tus

1 Come and seek the ways of Wis - dom, she who
2 Lis - ten to the voice of Wis - dom, cry - ing
3 Sis - ter Wis - dom, come, as - sist us; nur - ture

Sa - - pi - en - ti - a O_____

danced when earth was new. Fol - low close - ly what she
in the mark - et - place. Hear the Word made flesh a -
all who seek re - birth. Spi - rit - guide and close com -

_____ vir - tus Sa - pi - en - ti - a

teach - es, for her words are right and true. Wis - dom
mong us, full of glo - ry, truth, and grace. When the
pan - ion, bring to light our sa - cred worth. Free us

O _____ Sa - pi - en - ti - a

clears the path of jus - tice, show-ing us what love must do.
word takes root and rip-ens, peace and right - eous-ness em - brace.
to be - come your peo-ple, ho - ly friends of God and earth.

Final Ending

Give me oil in my lamp

burn - ing 'til the break of day.
seek - ing 'til the break of day.
sing - ing 'til the break of day.
serv - ing 'til the break of day.

Refrain

Sing ho - sa - na, sing ho - san - na,

sing ho - san - na to the King of Kings! King!

Words: Anonymous
Music: Arr. Betty Pulkingham © 1974 Celebration. All rights reserved. Used by permission.

62
O fiery Spirit

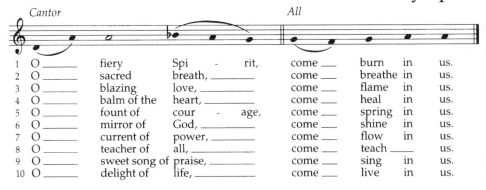

1	O _____	fiery	Spi - rit,	come __	burn	in	us.
2	O _____	sacred	breath, _____	come __	breathe	in	us.
3	O _____	blazing	love, _____	come __	flame	in	us.
4	O _____	balm of the	heart, _____	come __	heal	in	us.
5	O _____	fount of	cour - age,	come __	spring	in	us.
6	O _____	mirror of	God, _____	come __	shine	in	us.
7	O _____	current of	power, _____	come __	flow	in	us.
8	O _____	teacher of	all, _____	come __	teach ____	us.
9	O _____	sweet song of	praise, _____	come __	sing	in	us.
10	O _____	delight of	life, _____	come __	live	in	us.

63
I cannot dance, O Love

1   I cannot dance, O Love, unless you lead me on.
I cannot leap in gladness unless you lift me up.
From love to love we circle, beyond all knowledge grow,
for when you lead we follow, to new worlds you can show.

2   Love is the music 'round us, we glide as birds in air,
entwining, soul and body, your wings hold us with care.
Your Spirit is the harpist and all your children sing;
her hands the currents 'round us, your love the golden strings.

3   O blessed Love, your circling unites us, God and soul.
From the beginning, your arms embrace and make us whole.
Hold us in steps of mercy from which you never part,
that we may know more fully the dances of your heart.

Some groups may wish to improvise music and dance for this text, or use for prayer or meditation.

Mary, when the angel's voice

64

1 Ma - ry, when the an - gel's voice called you high - ly fa - vored,
2 Jo - seph, in your dark - est night, an - gel mes - sage hear - ing,
3 Old and sage E - liz - a - beth, birth an - ti - ci - pat - ing,
4 God whose name we mag - ni - fy, all your child - ren mat - ter.

dread and joy in your heart mixed, pon - dered there and sa - vored.
you cast not your love a - side, scorn and an - ger fear - ing.
nur - tur - ing your cous - in's will, you taught hope - ful wait - ing.
From op - pres - sion raise the poor; proud and might - y scat - ter.

May we learn to wel - come all that our life is bring - ing,
When a loved one brings us grief, rips our world a - sun - der,
So, as wo - men long have done, may we nev - er fal - ter
Seeds be - neath the win - ter snow live, 'tho all seems bar - ren.

e - ven when in pain we feel birth with - in us spring - ing.
dream - er, may we have your heart, o - pen to God's won - der.
to ex - tend a gen - tle touch, fears to cour - age al - ter.
Lift a car - ol, sing of hope for the Rose of Shar - on.

Words: Carol Goodwin King © 1997 Carol Goodwin King. All rights reserved. Used by permission.
Music: *Tempus adest floridum*, melody from *Piae Cantiones*, 1582; harm. Tom Whittemore © Tom Whittemore. All
          rights reserved. Used by permission.

65

Rejoice for martyrs strong

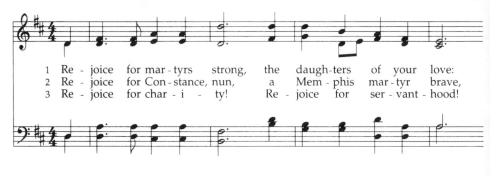

1 Re - joice for mar - tyrs strong, the daugh-ters of your love:
2 Re - joice for Con - stance, nun, a Mem - phis mar - tyr brave,
3 Re - joice for char - i - ty! Re - joice for ser - vant - hood!

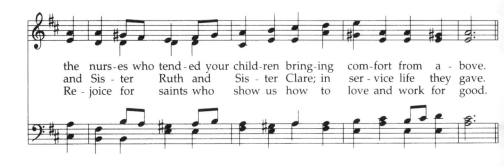

the nurs-es who tend-ed your child-ren bring-ing com-fort from a - bove.
and Sis - ter Ruth and Sis - ter Clare; in ser - vice life they gave.
Re - joice for saints who show us how to love and work for good.

Lift up your heart, lift up your voice, re - joice; a - gain I

say, re-joice, re - joice, a - gain I say: re - joice!

Words: Lisa Neufeld Thomas © 1999 Lisa Neufeld Thomas. All rights reserved. Used by permission.
Music: *Mayfair*, Frances McCollin (1892-1960).

Rejoice for Florence

66

1 Re - joice for Flor - ence, nurse, a daugh-ter of your love
2 Re - joice for cha - ri - ty, re - joice for serv - ant - hood.

a wo-man who tend-ed your chil - dren bring-ing com-fort from a - bove.
Re - joice for those who show us how to love and work for good.

Lift up your heart, lift up your voice, re - joice; a - gain I

say, re-joice, re - joice, a - gain I say: re - joice!

Words: Lisa Neufeld Thomas © 2001 Lisa Neufeld Thomas. All rights reserved. Used by permission.
Music: *Mayfair*, Frances McCollin (1892-1960).

Crashing waters at creation

1 Crash - ing wa - ters at cre - a - tion, or - dered
2 (Part - ing) wa - ter stood and trem - bled as the
3 (Cleans-ing) wa - ter once at Jor - dan closed a -

by the Spir - it's breath, first to wit - ness day's be -
cap - tives passed on through, wash-ing off the chains of
round the one fore - told, o - pened to re - veal the

gin - ning from the bright - ness of night's death. 2 Part - ing
bond - age chan-nel to a life made new. 3 Cleans-ing
glo - ry ev - er new and ev - er old. 4 Liv - ing

optional Descant

Liv-ing wa-ter, nev-er end - ing,_____ quench the thirst and

wa - ter, nev - er end - ing, quench the thirst and flood the

flood the soul. Well-spring, source of life e - ter - nal, drench our

soul. Well-spring, source of life e - ter - nal, drench our

dry - ness, make us whole, drench our dry - ness, make us

dry - ness, make us whole, drench our dry - ness, make us

whole.

whole.

Words: Sylvia G. Dunstan (1955-1993) © 1991 GIA Publications, Inc. All rights reserved. Used by permission.
Music: *Ellerman*, Sharon Marion Hershey © 1998 Harvestcross Productions. All rights reserved.
        Used by permission.
You must contact GIA Publications to reproduce these words, and Sharon Marion Hershey to reproduce this music.

We bring our children

68

1 We bring our children, Lord, to-day
2 On their be-half and in their name
3 Help us in all our ways to show

as once they did in Gal-i-lee,
our own com-mit-ment we re-new,
these grow-ing souls your truth and grace,

em-brace them with your love, we pray,
with them we die to sin and shame,
till they shall come them-selves to know

and bless each home and fam-i-ly.
with them we live a-gain in you.
the beau-ty of our Fa-ther's face.

Words: Elizabeth Cosnett © 1987 Stainer and Bell Ltd. (admin. Hope Publishing Company, Carol Stream, IL 60188).
         All rights reserved. Used by permission.
Music: *Angelus*, adapt. Georg Joseph, *Heilige Seelenlust*, Breslau, 1657.
You must contact Hope Publishing Company to reproduce these words.

We praise you, Lord

1 We praise you, Lord, for Je - sus Christ who died and
2 We praise you that this child now shares the free - dom
3 We praise you, Lord, that now this child is graft - ed
4 We praise you, Lord, for Je - sus Christ; he loves this

rose a - gain; he lives to break the pow'r of
Christ can give, has died to sin with Christ, and
to the vine, is made a mem - ber of your
child we bring: he frees, for - gives, and heals us

sin, and o - ver death to reign.
now with Christ is raised to live.
house and bears the cross as sign.
all, he lives and reigns as King.

One small child

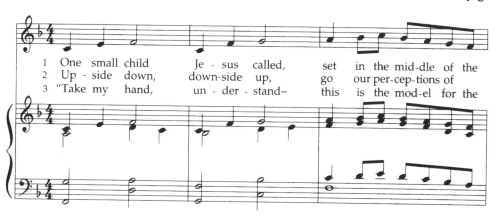

1 One small child Je - sus called, set in the mid-dle of the
2 Up - side down, down-side up, go our per-cep-tions of
3 "Take my hand, un - der - stand– this is the mod-el for the

grown-ups' cir - cle: "Wel - come him, Wel - come her, and
who's the great - est: "Take my word, trust my word as
king - dom peo - ple. Blessed are you, all of you who

then you are wel - com - ing me."
read - i - ly as this small child."
come to me like this small child."

close, in faith I root and grow

a - tor, source of ev - 'ry breath,
grain of life, and grape of love,
that in faith I root and grow

un - til I flow'r, un - til I

you are my rain, my wind, my sun.
your ve - ry bo - dy for my peace.
un - til I flow'r, un - til I (know.)

know. Moth - er - ing God Moth - er - ing God.

know. Moth - er - ing God.

72   **Mothering God**

1 Moth - er - ing God, you gave me birth in the bright morn - ing of this world. Cre - a - tor, source of ev - 'ry breath, you are my rain, my wind, my sun.

2 Moth - er - ing Christ, you took my form, of - fer - ing me your food of light, grain of life, and grape of love, your ver - y bod - y for my peace.

3 Moth - er - ing Spi - rit, nur - tur - ing one, in arms of pa - tience hold me close, so that in faith I root and grow un - til I flow - er, un - til I know.

Break thou the bread of life

73

Words: Mary A. Lathbury (1841-1913).
Music: William F. Sherwin (1826-1888).

1 O wheat whose crush-ing was for bread, O
2 O fruit whose crush-ing was for wine, O
3 O life whose crush-ing was for love, O

bread whose break-ing is for life, O life, your seem-ing end is
wine whose flow-ing is for blood, O blood, your pour-ing out is
love whose spend-ing was to death, O death, your mourn-ing is our

seed, a seed for wheat, our bread and life.
life, our life in you, O fruit-ful vine.
joy, full joy and birth to last-ing life.

1 Those who la - bor for the Lord,
2 Here the ban - quet now is laid,
3 Take the bread of hea - ven now,

here _____ come, to find their rest.
and _____ here the feast is set.
and _____ taste the glo - rious wine.

All can have the wel - come saved
Here the hun - gry heart is fed,
Go, re - freshed, your spi - rit blessed,

for _____ ev - ery wear - y guest.
and _____ here the Christ is met.
re - mem - b'ring Christ's de - sign.

We stand within the circle

1 We stand with-in the cir - cle of Christ's e - ter - nal light.
2 We live by faith he gives us, our food the bread and wine.
3 We sing with shin - ing voic - es, made wor - thy by his light.

No more to walk in dark - ness, no more to live by sight.
And ev - er lift our prais - es be - yond life's earth - ly signs.
Ho - san - na in the high - est, Christ, morn-ing's star burns bright.

Lord God, revealed

1 Lord God, re - vealed in gifts of bread and wine,
2 In Christ we find the self we long to be;
3 O en - ter Lord, and deign to be our guest,

our hun - gry hearts will ev - er lead us here
trust - ing his grace to find the hope un - tried;
we lin - ger not for com - fort now a - chieved;

to taste this food made by your love di - vine,
his strength be - comes our strength e - ter - nal - ly
speak to our spi - rits, Lord we leave re - freshed,

love spent for love's sake, we do now re - vere.
and in be - liev - ing we are sanc - ti - fied.
send - ing us forth your bless - ing now re - ceived.

Let us talents and tongues employ

1 Let us tal-ents and tongues em-ploy, reach-ing out with a shout of joy:
2 Christ is a-ble to make us one, at his ta-ble he sets the tone,
3 Je-sus calls us in, sends us out bear-ing fruit in a world of doubt,

bread is brok-en, the wine is poured, Christ is spok-en and seen and heard:
teach-ing peo-ple to live to bless, love in word and in deed ex-press:
gives us love to tell, bread to share: God Em-man-u-el ev-ery-where:

Je-sus lives a-gain, earth can breathe a-gain, pass the word a-round: loaves a-bound.

Words: Fred Kaan © 1975 Hope Publishing Company, Carol Stream, IL 60188. All rights reserved. Used by permission.
Music: *Linstead,* Jamaican folk song; adapt. Doreen Potter (1925-1980) © Hope Publishing Company, Carol Stream, IL 60188. All rights reserved. Used by permission.
You must contact Hope Publishing Company to reproduce this selection.

Bread of life

Refrain

Bread of life, hope of the world,

Je-sus Christ, our bro-ther: __ feed us now, give us life,

lead us __ to one an-oth-er. one an-oth-er. _____

| 1.–4. | to Verses | Final |

1. As we proclaim your death, as we recall your life,
2. The bread we break and share was scattered once as grain:
3. We eat this living bread, we drink this saving cup;
4. Hold us in unity, in love for all to see:
5. You are the bread of peace, you are the wine of joy,

we remember your promise
just as now it is gathered,
sign of hope in our broken world,
that the world may believe in you,
broken now for your people,

to return again.
make your people one.
source of lasting love.
God of all who live.
poured in endless love.

Je - sus, name a-bove all names, beau-ti-ful sav - iour, glo-rious

Lord; _____ Em - man - u - el— God __ is

with us, bless-ed Re - deem - er, liv - ing word.

Words and Music: Naida Hearn; arr. James Whitbourn © 1974 Scripture in Song (admin. Integrity Music/ASCAP, c/o Integrity Media, Inc., 1000 Cody Road, Mobile, AL. 36695). All rights reserved. Used by permission.

1 Just as I am, with - out ___ one plea
2 Just as I am, though tos - sed a - bout
3 Just as I am, poor, wretch - ed, blind;
4 Just as I am, thou wilt ___ re - ceive,
5 Just as I am, thy love ___ un - known
6 Just as I am, of that ___ free love

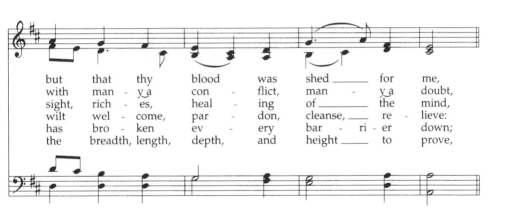

but that thy blood was shed ___ for me,
with man - y a con - flict, man - y a doubt,
sight, rich - es, heal - ing of ___ the mind,
has bro - ken ev - ery bar - ri - er down;
the breadth, length, depth, and height ___ to prove,

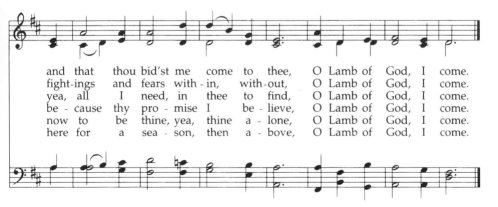

and that thou bid'st me come to thee, O Lamb of God, I come.
fight-ings and fears with - in, with-out, O Lamb of God, I come.
yea, all I need, in thee to find, O Lamb of God, I come.
be - cause thy pro - mise I be - lieve, O Lamb of God, I come.
now to be thine, yea, thine a - lone, O Lamb of God, I come.
here for a sea - son, then a - bove, O Lamb of God, I come.

Words: Charlotte Elliott (1789-1871).
Music: *Saffron Walden*, A.H. Brown (1830-1926).

Just as I am

1 Just as I am, with - out one plea
2 Just as I am, though tossed a - bout
3 Just as I am, poor, wretch - ed, blind;
4 Just as I am, thou wilt re - ceive,
5 Just as I am, thy love un - known
6 Just as I am, of that free love

but that thy blood was shed for me, ____
with many a con - flict, many a doubt, __
sight, rich - es, heal - ing of the mind, __
wilt wel - come, par - don, cleanse, re - lieve: __
has brok - en ev - ery bar - rier down; __
the breadth, length, depth, and height to prove, __

and that thou bid'st me come to thee, ____
fight - ings and fears with - in, with - out, ____
yea, all I need, in thee to find, ____
be - cause thy pro - mise I be - lieve, ____
now to be thine, yea, thine a - lone, ____
here for a sea - son, then a - bove, ____

O Lamb ____ of God, I come.

Words: Charlotte Elliott (1789-1871).
Music: *Misericordia*, Henry Smart (1813-1879).

Just as I am

1 Just as I am, with - out one plea,
2 Just as I am, though tossed a - bout
3 Just as I am, poor, wretch - ed, blind;
4 Just as I am: thou wilt re - ceive;
5 Just as I am, thy love un - known
6 Just as I am, of thy great love

but that thy blood was shed for me,
with man - y a con - flict, man - y a doubt;
sight, rich - es, heal - ing of the mind,
wilt wel - come, par - don, cleanse, re - lieve;
has bro - ken ev - ery bar - rier down;
the breadth, length, depth, and height to prove,

and that thou bidd'st me come to thee,
fight - ings and fears with - in, with - out,
yea, all I need, in thee to find,
be - cause thy prom - ise I be - lieve,
now to be thine, yea, thine a - lone,
here for a sea - son, then a - bove:

O Lamb of God, I come, I come.

Words: Charlotte Elliott (1789-1871).
Music: *Woodworth*, William B. Bradbury (1816-1868).

85   Circle the table

1 Cir-cle the ta - ble, hands now ex - tend. Wel-come a stran - ger,
2 See on the ta - ble, set in Christ's name, signs of the suf - fering
3 Eat and be thank - ful, lift up your praise. God has for-giv - en

greet a new friend. O-pen your cir - cle, let it ex - pand.
love ov-er-came: cup of sweet wine and loaf of fine bread.
your self-ish ways. Go from the ta - ble, go forth to share

1. 2. | **3.**

Wel-come God's child-ren from far a - way lands.
All things are rea - dy so come and be fed.
with your new neigh-bors the   love you found there.

God of all time

86

1 God of all time, all sea-sons of our liv - ing,
2 Here in this place, where oth - ers have been build - ing,
3 Spi - rit who draws our fra - gile selves to - geth - er,
4 Let us not die from pov - er - ty of car - ing,

source of our spark, pro - tec - tor of our flame,
we come to claim the leg - a - cy of faith,
Spi - rit who turns a strang-er to a friend,
let us not starve, where love is to be shared.

blaz - ing be - fore our birth, be - yond our dy - ing,
take, in our turn the tell - ing of your sto - ry,
be at this ta - ble where we greet each o - ther,
Come, break us o - pen to re - ceive your heal - ing:

God of all time, we come to sing your name.
and, though we trem - ble, speak your hope, your truth.
be in the peace we pass from hand to hand.
your bro - ken bod - y be our wine and bread.

All who hunger gather gladly

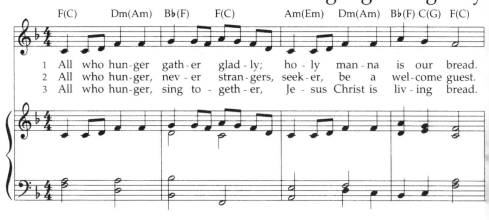

1 All who hun-ger gath-er glad-ly; ho-ly man-na is our bread.
2 All who hun-ger, nev-er stran-gers, seek-er, be a wel-come guest.
3 All who hun-ger, sing to-geth-er, Je-sus Christ is liv-ing bread.

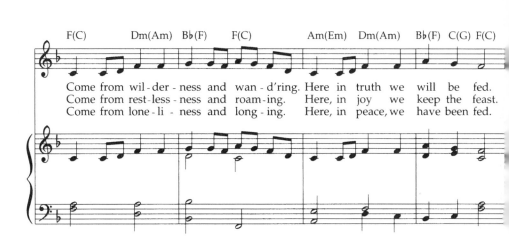

Come from wil-der-ness and wan-d'ring. Here in truth we will be fed.
Come from rest-less-ness and roam-ing. Here, in joy we keep the feast.
Come from lone-li-ness and long-ing. Here, in peace, we have been fed.

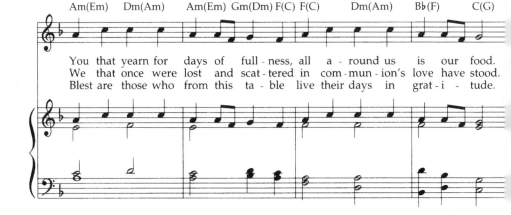

You that yearn for days of full-ness, all a-round us is our food.
We that once were lost and scat-tered in com-mun-ion's love have stood.
Blest are those who from this ta-ble live their days in grat-i-tude.

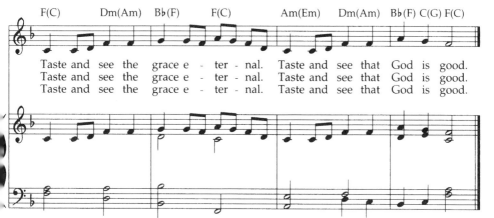

Taste and see the grace e - ter - nal. Taste and see that God is good.
Taste and see the grace e - ter - nal. Taste and see that God is good.
Taste and see the grace e - ter - nal. Taste and see that God is good.

Nada te turbe 88

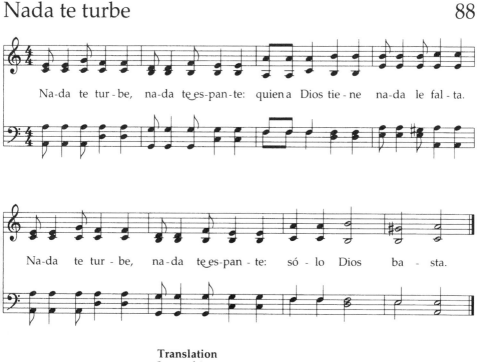

Na-da te tur - be, na-da te_es-pan - te: quien a Dios tie - ne na-da le fal - ta.

Na-da te tur - be, na-da te_es-pan - te: só - lo Dios ba - sta.

Translation
Let nothing worry or upset you:
whoever has God needs fear nothing.
Let nothing worry or upset you:
God alone is enough.

We gather at your table, Lord

1 We gath-er at your ta-ble, Lord: we hum-bly lift our
2 We share this meal and we are fed. Such bas-ic gifts be-
3 God, pour your Spi-rit on us all, and on these gifts that
4 From north and south, from west and east, now rec-on-ciled, we

hearts to you! Here all are wel-comed, all re-stored, and
come your sign: we see you bro-ken in the bread; we
we re-ceive; for in Christ's pre-sence we re-call his
ga-ther near; we taste your king-dom's ban-quet feast, so

For canon only

all are giv-en work to do. (-en work to do.)
know your love in com-mon wine. (in com-mon wine.)
life and death, and so be-lieve. (and so be-lieve.)
find-ing strength to serve you here. (to serve you here.)

Words: Carolyn Winfrey Gillette © 1999 Carolyn Winfrey Gillette, from *Gifts of Love: New Hymns for Today's Worship* (Geneva Press 2000). All rights reserved. Used by permission.
Music: *The Eighth Tune*, Thomas Tallis (1505?-1585).

God of freedom

90

1 God of free-dom, God of jus-tice, you whose love is strong as death,
2 Rid the earth of tor-ture's ter-ror, you whose hands were nailed to wood;
3 Make in us a cap-tive con-science quick to hear, to act, to plead;

you who saw the dark of pri-son, you who knew the price of faith—
hear the cries of pain and pro-test, you who shed the tears and blood—
make us tru-ly sis-ters, bro-thers, of what-ev - er race or creed—

touch our world of sad op-pres-sion with your Spi-rit's heal-ing breath.
move in us the power of pi - ty rest-less for the com-mon good.
teach us to be ful - ly hu-man, o - pen to each oth-er's needs.

* Optional for last verse.

Words: Shirley Erena Murray © 1992 Hope Publishing Company, Carol Stream, IL 60188. All rights reserved. Used
by permission.
Music: *Libertad*, Robert A.M. Ross © 2001 Ralamar Sparks Enterprises. Used by permission. All rights reserved.
You must contact Hope Publishing Company to reproduce these words.

Heal me, Lord

Part I

1 Heal me, Lord,   heal me, Lord,   heal me,
    am,   here I am,   here I
    you,   touch-ing you,   touch-ing
    Lord,   thank you, Lord,   thank you,

Part II

1, 2, 3 in your mer-cy   in your mer-cy
4   for your mer-cy   for your mer-cy

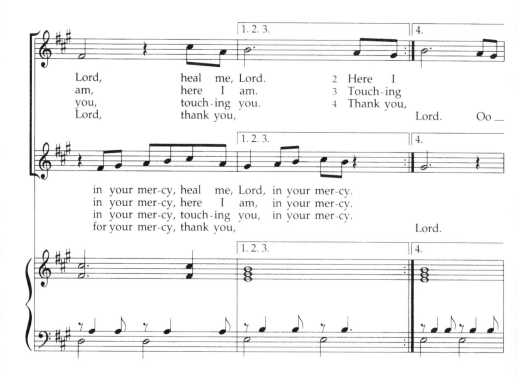

Lord,   heal me, Lord.   2 Here I
am,   here I am.   3 Touch-ing
you,   touch-ing you.   4 Thank you,
Lord,   thank you,   Lord.   Oo —

in your mer-cy, heal me, Lord, in your mer-cy.
in your mer-cy, here I am, in your mer-cy.
in your mer-cy, touch-ing you, in your mer-cy.
for your mer-cy, thank you,   Lord.

Oo

Be still and know that I am God

The part numbered 1 should be sung alone and repeated several times. Then the parts numbered 2, 3 and 4 are added one at a time repeating each new group several times before the next part enters. There is no end to the tune, and you may continue as long as forever, or bring the parts out in reverse order (4-3-2-1) for a tidier finish.

1 God, cre - a - tor, source of heal - ing here we
2 Je - sus, known to friend and seek - er ex - er -
3 Ho - ly Spi - rit, bring us whole-ness, come with
4 Tri - ni - ty of awe and won - der yours the

pray for whole-ness and health. Guide our work, our
cis - ing heal - er's art, may the strong sup -
your trans - form - ing love; give us free - dom,
glo - ry, yours the praise. Strike our bind - ing

thoughts, and feel - ing, guide the shar - ing of our wealth.
port the weak-er show - ing love with head and heart;
hope and bold-ness, raise our eyes to see from a - bove;
chains a - sun - der, lib - er - ate our cramp-ing ways.

Give dis - cern - ment in our de - ci - sions give com -
give fresh en - er - gy and pur - pose when un -
shape our sys - tems, in - sti - tu - tions, clar - i -
May our lives re - flect your splend-our, in a -

pas - sion	in	our	care;	rec - on - cile	our
rea - son - ing	blocks	your	grace,	spare	us	harm,	in
fy	our	blind - ed	sight,	as	we	seek	God -
bun - dance	Lord	we	ask.	God,	our	guide	and

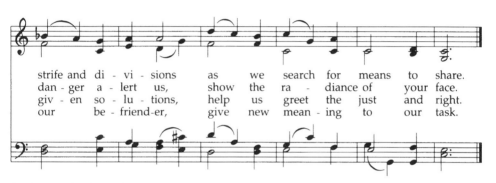

strife and di - vi - sions	as	we	search for means	to	share.
dan - ger a - lert us,	show	the	ra - diance of	your	face.
giv - en so - lu - tions,	help	us	greet the just	and	right.
our	be - friend-er,	give	new	mean - ing	to	our	task.

In boldness, look to God

Fm(Em)　Db(C)　Eb(D)　Ab(G)　Fm(Em)　Db(C)

1 In bold-ness, look to　God for help, like wo - men folk who
2 In bold-ness, lean on　God for strength, and heal-ing from dis -
3 In bold-ness, learn of　God the truth of Ma - ry's bet - ter
4 In bold-ness, love, nor count the cost. Con - front the world's harsh

Ab(G)　Bbm(Am)　Eb(D)　Ab(G)

dared: to ask that Je - sus heal a child, that
ease, of mind and bod - y, heart and will, whose
part: by fear and cen - sure un - de - terred, de -
stare: like one who washed the feet of Christ, and

Fm(Em)　Db(C)　Eb(D)　Fm(Em)　Ab(G)　Bb(Am)

crumbs of grace be shared, that out - cast ones be
bond - age Je - sus frees. Reach out and touch the
ter - mined in her heart to kneel at Je - sus'
wiped them with her hair, poured per - fume to a -

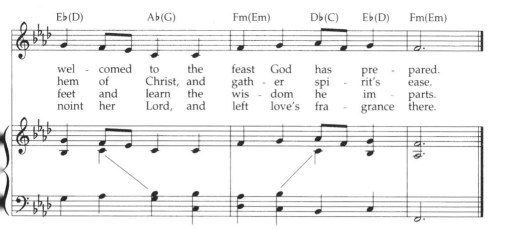

wel - comed   to   the   feast   God   has   pre - pared.
hem   of   Christ, and   gath - er   spi - rit's ease.
feet   and   learn   the   wis - dom   he   im -   parts.
noint   her   Lord,   and   left   love's fra - grance there.

A long lost lamb

gain,   most lov - ing - ly   re - ceived._____
tears   has put   be - hind   her past._____   Good news! It's
light   and mourns his ar -   ro - gance._____
God,   for love   a - waits   you there._____

time   to ce - le - brate with friends who ga - ther round._____

So God   re - joic - es,   Je - sus said,   when-

1. 2. 3.   4.

e'er   the   lost is   found!_____ 2 The   found!____
                                          3 The
                                          4 Let

Words: Mary Nelson Keithahn © 1996 Abingdon Press (admin. The Copyright Company, Nashville, TN). All rights
         reserved. International copyright secured. Used by permission.
Music: Carl Haywood © 2002 Carl Haywood. All rights reserved. Used by permission.
You must contact Carl Haywood to reproduce this music.

1 Heal-ing riv - er of the Spi - rit, bathe the wounds that liv - ing brings.
2 Well-spring of the heal-ing Spi - rit, stream that flows to bring re - lease,
3 Liv - ing stream that heals the na - tions, make us chan - nels of your pow'r.

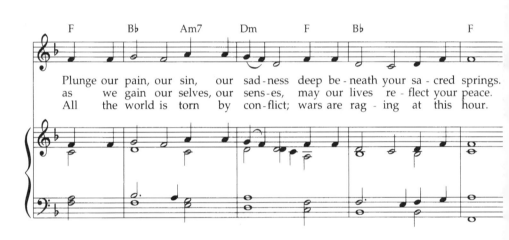

Plunge our pain, our sin, our sad-ness deep be - neath your sa - cred springs.
as we gain our selves, our sens-es, may our lives re - flect your peace.
All the world is torn by con-flict; wars are rag - ing at this hour.

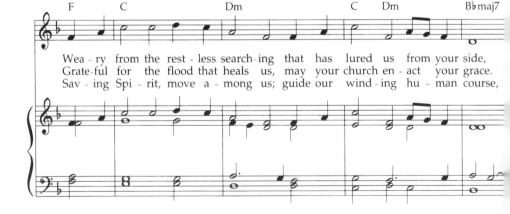

Wea - ry from the rest - less search-ing that has lured us from your side,
Grate-ful for the flood that heals us, may your church en - act your grace.
Sav - ing Spi - rit, move a - mong us; guide our wind - ing hu - man course,

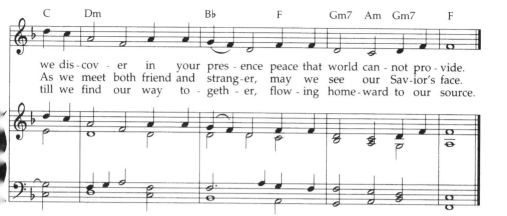

we dis-cov - er in your pres - ence peace that world can - not pro - vide.
As we meet both friend and strang-er, may we see our Sav-ior's face.
till we find our way to - geth - er, flow - ing home-ward to our source.

Words: Ruth C. Duck, from *Circles of Care: Hymns and Song* © 1996 The Pilgrim Press. All rights reserved.
          Used by permission.
Music: *Beach Spring,* from *The Sacred Harp*, Philadelphia, 1844 © 1978 *Lutheran Book of Worship* (admin. Augsburg
          Fortress Publishers). All rights reserved. Used by permission.
You must contact Augsburg Fortress Publishers to reproduce this music.

In deepest night

1 In deep-est night, in dark-est days, when harps are hung, no
2 When friend was lost, when love de-ceived, dear Je-sus wept, God
3 When through the wa-ters winds our path, a-round us pain, a-

songs we raise, when si-lence must suf-fice as praise, yet
was be-reaved; so with us in our grief God grieves, and
round us death: deep calls to deep, a sav-ing breath, and

1. 2. | **3.**

sound-ing in us qui-et-ly there is the song of God.
round a-bout us mourn-ful-ly there are the tears of God.
found be-side us faith-ful-ly there is the love of God.

Words: Susan Palo Cherwein, from *O Blessed Spring* © 1995 Augsburg Fortress Publishers. Used by Permission. All rights reserved.
Music: Emily Maxson Porter, from *O Blessed Spring* © 1997 Augsburg Fortress Publishers. All rights reserved. Used by permission.
You must contact Augsburg Fortress Publishers to reproduce this selection.

Lord, speak to me

98

1 Lord, speak to me, that I may speak in
2 O lead me, Lord, that I may lead the
3 O teach me, Lord, that I may teach the

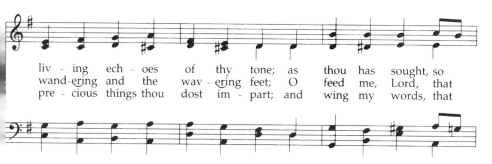

liv - ing ech - oes of thy tone; as thou has sought, so
wand-'ring and the wav - 'ring feet; O feed me, Lord, that
pre - cious things thou dost im - part; and wing my words, that

let me seek thy err - ing child - ren lost and lone.
I may feed thy hun - gry ones with man - na sweet.
they may reach the hid - den depths of many a heart.

Words: Frances R. Havergal (1836-1879).
Music: *Canonbury*, adapt. Robert A. Schumann (1810-1856), from *Nachtstüke*, 1839; arr. from *Hymnal with Tunes, Old and New*, 1872.

1 In the name of Christ we gath - er, in the name of
2 Sons and daugh-ters of the Spi - rit these are called to
3 In the min - is - try of preach-ing may the Word spring
4 Now with - in this sol - emn mo - ment we in - voke the
5 Word of joy, en - liv - ening Spi - rit, more than lov - er,

Christ we sing! Ce - le - brate new vows, new prom - ise
teach and care, called as were the first dis - ci - ples,
in - to life, in the time of doubt and chal - lenge
power of God by the hands laid on in bless - ing
par - ent, friend, born in Je - sus, born in Ma - ry,

of a life's whole of - fer - ing, here or - dained to
com - mon - wealth of Christ to share, by the bread and
may its truth af - firm be - lief, in the day of
be there strength to take the load, be there faith - ful -
born in us, that love ex - tend, grow with - in your

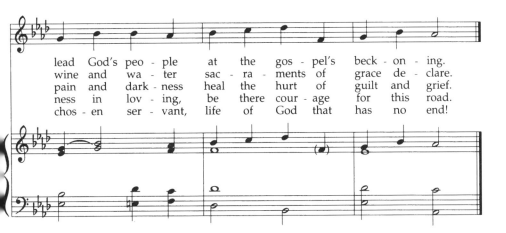

lead God's peo - ple at the gos - pel's beck - on - ing.
wine and wa - ter sac - ra - ments of grace de - clare.
pain and dark - ness heal the hurt of guilt and grief.
ness in lov - ing, be there cour - age for this road.
chos - en ser - vant, life of God that has no end!

100

Be a shepherd for my flock

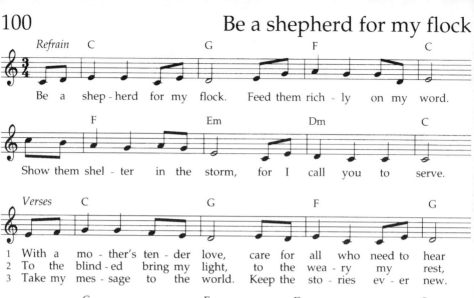

Refrain

Be a shep - herd for my flock. Feed them rich - ly on my word.
Show them shel - ter in the storm, for I call you to serve.

Verses

1. With a mo - ther's ten - der love, care for all who need to hear
2. To the blind - ed bring my light, to the wea - ry my rest,
3. Take my mes - sage to the world. Keep the sto - ries ev - er new.

they can run in - to my arms. Ease ev - ery fear.
to the poor a - bun-dant life for - ev - er blest.
Sing my truth, dance my joy. I'll car - ry you.

101

Imela

I - me - la, i - me - la, i - me - la, O - ka - ka.

I - me - la, Chi - ne - ke. I - me - la On - y'o - ma.

Translation
Thank you, great God.
Thank you because you are good.

Creator of all time and space 102

1 Cre - a - tor of all time and space, we read your
2 We thank you for the hu - man mind, in mys - tic
3 O God of plan - et, moon, and sun, we won - der,
4 For mir - a - cles as large as space, as small as

im - age on each face. Great Spir - it of the
har - mo - ny de - signed, for word and im - age,
know - ing all you've done, that you be - friend the
cells, as deep as grace, we of - fer you our

cos - mic whole, you made us bod - y, mind, and soul.
dream and thought, for les - sons learned and an - swers sought.
hu - man race, and fill our lives with love and grace.
thanks and praise, and pledge to serve you all our days.

Words: Ruth C. Duck, from *Circles of Care: Hymns and Song* © 1996 The Pilgrim Press. All rights reserved.
        Used by permission.
Music: *Conditor alme siderum*, plainsong, Mode 4; acc. Bruce Neswick © 2002 Bruce Neswick. All rights reserved.
        Used by permission.

Media sida

me - di - me ho - nam, me - di - me ho - nam, me - di - me ho - nam nyi - naa,
meh - dee - meh hoh - nahm, meh - dee - meh hoh - nahm, meh - dee - meh hoh - nahm nyee - nah,

Fine (last time cut off on downbeat)

me - yi mi po - fo - na yeo. _____
meh - yee mee pō - foh - nah yoh. _____

As - see se me - yi naa yo o say ye yio, _____
Ah - seh seh meh - yee nah yoh oh sah yeh _ yoh, _____

D.S. al Fine

as - see se me - da naa - si o - san - da - sio.
ah - seh seh meh - dyah nah - see oh - sahn - dah - syoh.

Translation
I will praise and exult my God for God's love is everlasting.
I will proclaim God's greatness to all nations.
Nurturing God, I give you praise!
I will glorify you at all times for you protect me from all harm.
I will exult, my God and give praise all my life.
All ought to give praise to God for God deserves praise.
All ought to give praise to God for God deserves thanksgiving.

n Africa, during an outdoor eucharistic liturgy, Media sida is sung as people bring fruits, grains, and other gifts to
he altar at the Offertory. It is accompanied by a talking drum. In the absence of this instrument, the accompaniment
nay be played on any small drum or other percussive instrument or it may be clapped.

Words: From the liturgy of southern Ghana.

104   Sing to the Lord

Laus Trinitati

O praise be to you Holy Trinity

105

The slurs indicate the chant flow in groups of twos and threes.

Bring many names

1 Bring man - y names, beau - ti - ful and good,
2 Strong mo - ther God, work - ing night and day,
3 Warm fa - ther God, hug - ging ev' - ry child,
4 Old, ach - ing God, grey with end - less care,
5 Young, grow - ing God, ea - ger, on the move,
6 Great, liv - ing God, nev - er ful - ly known,

ce - le - brate in par - a - ble and sto - ry,
plan - ning all the won - ders of cre - a - tion,
feel - ing all the strains of hu - man liv - ing,
calm - ly pierc - ing e - vil's new dis - guis - es,
say - ing no to false - hood and un - kind - ness,
joy - ful dark - ness far be - yond our see - ing,

ho - li - ness in glo - ry, liv - ing, lov - ing God.
set - ting each e - qua - tion, gen - i - us at play:
car - ing and for - giv - ing till we're re - con - ciled:
glad of good sur - pris - es, wis - er than des - pair:
cry - ing out for jus - tice, giv - ing all you have:
clos - er yet than breath - ing, ev - er - last - ing home:

Hail and ho-san-na! Hail and ho-san-na, bring man-y names!
Hail and ho-san-na! Hail and ho-san-na, strong mo-ther God!
Hail and ho-san-na! Hail and ho-san-na, warm fa-ther God!
Hail and ho-san-na! Hail and ho-san-na, old, ach-ing God!
Hail and ho-san-na! Hail and ho-san-na, young, grow-ing God!
Hail and ho-san-na! Hail and ho-san-na, great, liv-ing God!

Words: Brian Wren © 1989, (rev.) 1994 Hope Publishing Company, Carol Stream, IL 60188. All rights reserved.
         Used by permission.
Music: Robert A.M. Ross © 1990 Ralamar Sparks Enterprises. All rights reserved. Used by permission.
You must contact Hope Publishing Company to reproduce this text.

Let all things now living

1 Let all things now liv-ing a song of thanks-giv-ing to
2 His law he en - for-ces, the stars in their cours-es and

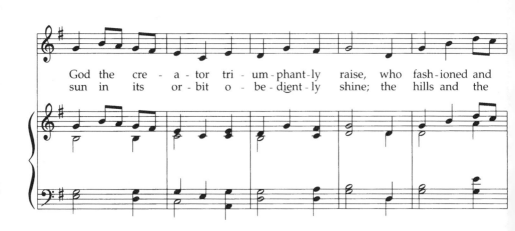

God the cre - a - tor tri - um-phant-ly raise, who fash-ioned and
sun in its or - bit o - be-dient-ly shine; the hills and the

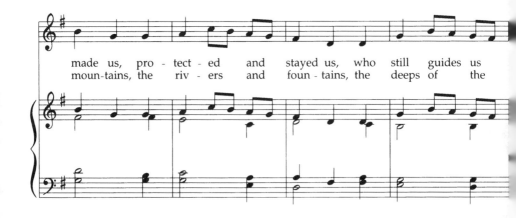

made us, pro - tect - ed and stayed us, who still guides us
moun-tains, the riv - ers and foun - tains, the deeps of the

To God be the glory

1 To God be the glo - ry, great things he has done! So loved he the
2 O per - fect re - demp-tion, the pur - chase of blood! To ev - ery be-
3 Great things he has taught us, great things he has done, and great our re-

world that he gave us his son, who yield - ed his life an a -
liev - er the pro - mise of God! The vil - est of - fen - der who
joic - ing through Je - sus the son; but pur - er and high - er and

tone-ment for sin and o - pened the life - gate that all may go in.
tru - ly be - lieves, that mo - ment from Je - sus for - give-ness re - ceives.
great-er will be our won - der, our rap - ture, when Je - sus we see.

Refrain

Praise the Lord! Praise the Lord! Let the earth hear his voice!

Praise the Lord! Praise the Lord! Let the peo - ple re - joice!

O come to the Fa - ther, through Je - sus the son,

and give him the glo - ry! Great things he has done!

Words: Fanny Crosby (1820-1915).
Music: W. H. Doane (1832-1916).

People of God

1 Peo - ple of God, ga - ther to - ge - ther, come, let us
2 Hear-ing God's word, heed-ing the mes - sage, come and re -
3 Bear-ing your gifts, en - ter God's pre - sence; come, let us
4 Wo - men and men, har - mo - ny blend - ing, come, swell the

sing on this glo - rious day. Shout-ing a - broad
joice as we an - swer the call. With one ac - cord,
share in the hea - ven - ly feast. Mend-ing all rifts,
cho - rus in lov - ing ac - cord. Rais - ing a - gain

praise to the Mak - er, come and with bo - dy and soul let us pray.
made in God's im - age, come in com - mu - ni - ty, wel - com-ing all.
heal - ing di - vi - sions, come and from sor - rows and hurts be re - leased.
thanks ne - ver end - ing, come to the God who is Wis - dom and Word.

Refrain

Come, let us join in the hea - ven - ly dance,

prais - ing in joy - ous ce - le - bra - tion.

Words: Patricia B. Clark © 2003 Selah Publishing Company, Inc. 58 Pearl Street, Kingston, NY 12402. www.selahpub.com. All rights reserved. Used by permission.

Music: *Earth and All Stars*, David N. Johnson © Augsburg Fortress Publishers. All rights reserved. Used by permission.

You must contact Selah Publishing Company to reproduce these words, and Augsburg Fortress Publishers to reproduce this music.

110

Dance and sing

May be sung with varied tempos, beginning slowly at m. 5 and gradually getting faster until the refrain.
Optional: tambourine on beats 1 and 3 to m. 5; then quarter notes to end.

111 All things bright and beautiful

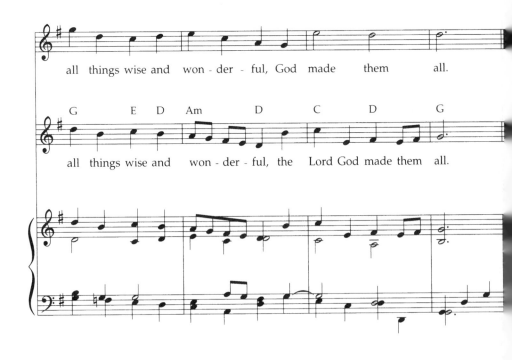

1 Each lit - tle flower that o - pens, each lit - tle bird that sings,
2 The pur - ple - head - ed moun - tain, the riv - er run - ning by,
3 The cold wind in the win - ter, the pleas - ant sum - mer sun,
4 He gave us eyes to see them, and lips that we might tell

Repeat Refrain

he made their glow - ing col - ors, he made their ti - ny wings.
the sun - set, and the morn - ing that bright - ens up the sky.
the ripe fruits in the gar - den, he made them ev - ery one.
how great is God Al - might - y, who has made all things well.

Words: Cecil Frances Alexander (1818-1895) © 1921 (ren.) J. Curwen & Sons Ltd. (admin. G. Schirmer, Inc. 257 Park
         Avenue South, NY, NY 10010). Used by Permission. All rights reserved.
Music: *Royal Oak*, melody from *The Dancing Master*, 1686; arr. and adapt. Martin Fallas Shaw (1875-1958) © J.
         Curwen & Sons Ltd. (admin. G. Schirmer, Inc., 257 Park Avenue South, NY, NY 10010); desc. Richard Proulx
         © 1979 GIA Publications, Inc. All rights reseved. Used by permission.
You must contact GIA Publications to reproduce this descant.

All things bright and beautiful

Refrain

All things bright and beau - ti - ful, all crea - tures great and small,

Fine

all things wise and won - der-ful, the Lord God made them all.

1 Each lit - tle flower that o - pens, each lit - tle bird that sings,
2 The pur - ple - head - ed moun - tain, the riv - er run - ning by,
3 The cold wind in the win - ter, the pleas-ant sum - mer sun,
4 He gave us eyes to see them, and lips that we might tell

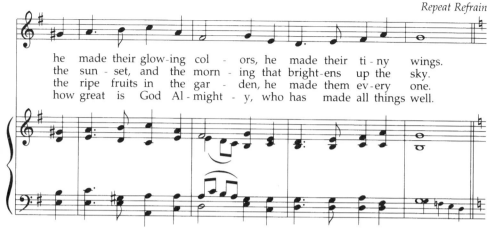

Repeat Refrain

he made their glow-ing col - ors, he made their ti - ny wings.
the sun - set, and the morn - ing that bright-ens up the sky.
the ripe fruits in the gar - den, he made them ev - ery one.
how great is God Al - might - y, who has made all things well.

Words: Cecil Frances Alexander (1818-1895) © 1921 (ren.) J. Curwen & Sons Ltd., (admin. G. Schirmer, Inc., 257 Park
         Avenue South, NY, NY 10010). Used by Permission. All rights reserved.
Music: *All Things Bright and Beautiful*, W.H. Monk (1823-1889).

113

Queremos cantar
We sing a new song

1 Que - re - mos can - tar, um hi - no a ti, Se - nhor, u - ma
2 Que - re - mos can - tar, a nos - sa gra - ti dão por
1 We sing a new song to you, cre - a - tor God, a new
2 We sing a new song to you, cre - a - tor Lord, for you

no - va can - ção que vem do co - ra - ção.
to - da be - le - za da tua cri - a - ção.
song from our hearts to bring our love and praise.
bring life to be - ing through the e - ter - nal word.

Pe - lo céu tão vas - to, o mar tão gran - de,
For the sky's so vast, the seas so wide, this

ção. A   ti can - ta - mos nos - sa gra - ti dão!_____
raised to   sing to you our thanks and our praise._____

114   Grateful praise

Grate-ful praise and hymns of a - do - ra - tion, blend our voic - es

in a hap-py throng.   Boun-teous days, a - live with ce - le - bra - tion,

lift   our   hearts to you in thanks-giv - ing song.

Sing hallelujah

115

Sing hallelujah

1 Sing hal - le - lu - jah to the Lord;
2 Lift up your hearts un - to the Lord;
3 Christ's re - sur - rec - tion sets us free;
4 There - fore we ce - le - brate the feast;

sing hal - le - lu - jah to the Lord.
lift up your hearts un - to the Lord.
Christ's re - sur - rec - tion sets us free.
there - fore we ce - le - brate the feast.

Sing hal-le-lu - jah,

sing hal-le-lu - jah,

sing hal - le - lu - jah to the Lord.
lift up your hearts un - to the Lord.
Christ's re - sur - rec - tion sets us free.
there - fore we cel - e - brate the feast.

Fine

116 Sing to celebrate the city!

1 Sing to ce - le - brate the ci - ty!
2 We who are the ci - ty's traf - fic,
3 Ce - le - brate the art of liv - ing!

Sing the lives of peo - ple there,
driv - ing, driv - en, keep-ing pace,
Ev - 'ry col - our, ev - 'ry sport,

sing the work of skill and beau - ty,
name the God who makes us neigh-bours,
ev - 'ry cul - ture's dance and mus - ic,

Fine

all   who   serve and   all   who   care.
gives our   faith   a   hu - man   face;
ev - 'ry   truth that   love has   taught.

In   the   dic - tates   of   the   dol - lar,
in   the   work-place   of   God's   peo - ple,
Be   for   God   with - in   the   ci - ty,

in   the   sys - tems where we   live,
in   the   high - rise   and   the   home
life   and   lov - ing   are   not   priced:

find the cur - ren - cy of kind - ness,
our a - gen - da is for jus - tice,
light the lights of joy - ful wor - ship,

D.C. al Fine

eyes to smile and hearts to give.
chang-ing lives for good to come.
set the ta - ble for the Christ! *(repeat Verse 1)*

D.C. al Fine

My soul gives glory to my God

1 My soul gives glo - ry to my God. My
2 My God has done great things for me: yes,
3 From age to age, to all who fear, such
4 Love casts the might - y from their thrones, pro -
5 Praise God, whose lov - ing cov - e - nant sup -

heart pours out its praise. God lift - ed up my
ho - ly is this name. All peo - ple will de -
mer - cy love im - parts, dis - pens - ing jus - tice
motes the in - se - cure, leaves hun - gry spi - rits
ports those in dis - tress, re - mem - ber - ing past

low - li - ness in man - y mar - vel - ous ways.
clare me blessed, and bless - ings they shall claim.
far and near, dis - miss - ing self - ish hearts.
sat - is - fied, the rich seem sud - den - ly poor.
prom - is - es with pres - ent faith - ful - ness.

1 What gift can we bring, what pres - ent, what to - ken?
2 Give thanks for the past, for those who had vi - sion,
3 Give thanks for to - mor - row, full of sur - pris - es,
4 This gift we now bring, this pres - ent, this to - ken,

What words can con - vey it the joy of this day?
who plant - ed and wa - tered so dreams could come true.
for know - ing what - ev - er to - mor - row may bring,
these words can con - vey it the joy of this day!

When grate - ful we come, re - mem - ber - ing, re - joic - ing,
Give thanks for the now, for stud - y for wor - ship,
God gives us his word that al - ways, for - ev - er,
When grate - ful we come, re - mem - ber - ing, re - joic - ing,

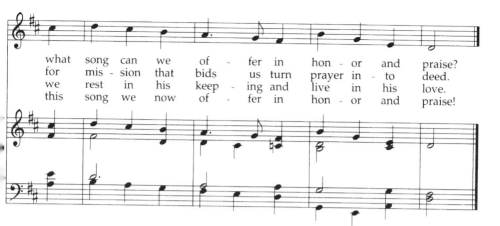

what song can we of - fer in hon - or and praise?
for mis - sion that bids us turn prayer in - to deed.
we rest in his keep - ing and live in his love.
this song we now of - fer in hon - or and praise!

119

Blessed assurance

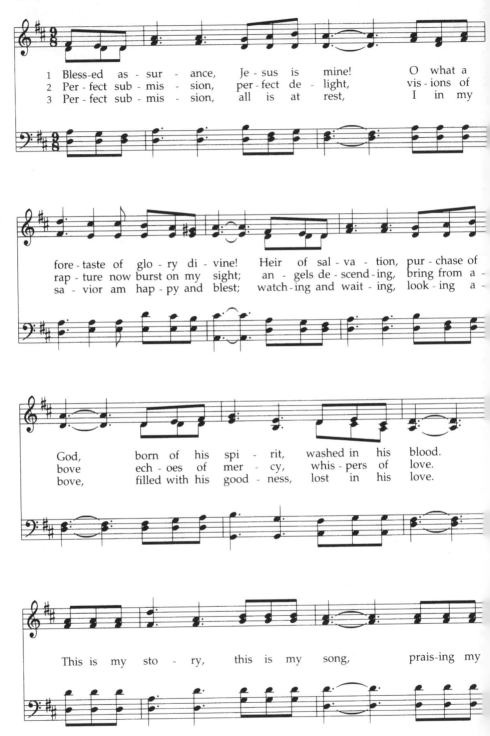

1 Bless-ed as - sur - ance, Je - sus is mine! O what a
2 Per - fect sub - mis - sion, per - fect de - light, vis - ions of
3 Per - fect sub - mis - sion, all is at rest, I in my

fore - taste of glo - ry di - vine! Heir of sal - va - tion, pur - chase of
rap - ture now burst on my sight; an - gels de - scend - ing, bring from a -
sa - vior am hap - py and blest; watch - ing and wait - ing, look - ing a -

God, born of his spi - rit, washed in his blood.
bove ech - oes of mer - cy, whis - pers of love.
bove, filled with his good - ness, lost in his love.

This is my sto - ry, this is my song, prais - ing my

sa - vior all the day long; this is my sto - ry, this is my

song,   prais-ing my sa - vior   all   the day   long.

Words: Fanny Crosby (1820-1915).
Music: Phoebe P. Knapp (1839-1908).

O God, we praise your holy name

O God, we praise your ho-ly name, as one in Christ we stand.

You've made us sis-ters through your son with kin in ev-ery land.

A-noint us now with your own grace that we might read-y be

to touch the world with gen-tle-ness as through Christ's eyes we see.

Oh, God, in joy we lift our song, your words we will pro - claim,

un - til the love we share to - day through-out the world shall reign.

Come, sing the joy of Miriam

1 Come, sing the joy of Mir - i - am, for she has seen dry land. Come, dance with her as now we join this grate - ful, glo - rious band.

2 Our faith - ful God de - liv - ers us when en - e - mies as - sail, the world will bring false prom - is - es. Our God will still pre - vail.

3 Come, jour - ney on with Mir - i - am, em - pow - ered, strong and free. Come, live our praise through all our days, serv - ing God's fam - i - ly.

Music: *Azmon*, Carl G. Gläser (1784-1829); adapt. and arr. Lowell Mason (1792-1872).

O Mary, don't you weep

O Ma-ry, don't you weep, don't you mourn, O Ma-ry, don't you

weep, don't you mourn; Pha-raoh's ar-my got drown-ded,

O Ma-ry, don't you weep.

1 Some of these morn - ings
2 When I get to hea-ven goin' to
3 When I get to hea-ven goin' to

bright and fair, take my wings and cleave the air.
sing and shout, no - bod-y there for turn me out.
put on my shoes, run a-bout glo - ry and tell all the news.

Pha-raoh's ar-my got drown-ded, O Ma-ry, don't you weep.

ords: Traditional
usic: Negro Spiritual; arr. John W. Work (1901-1967), from *American Negro Songs and Spirituals* © 1940, 1968 Crown Publishers. Used by permission of Bonanza Books, a division of Random House. All rights reserved.

123

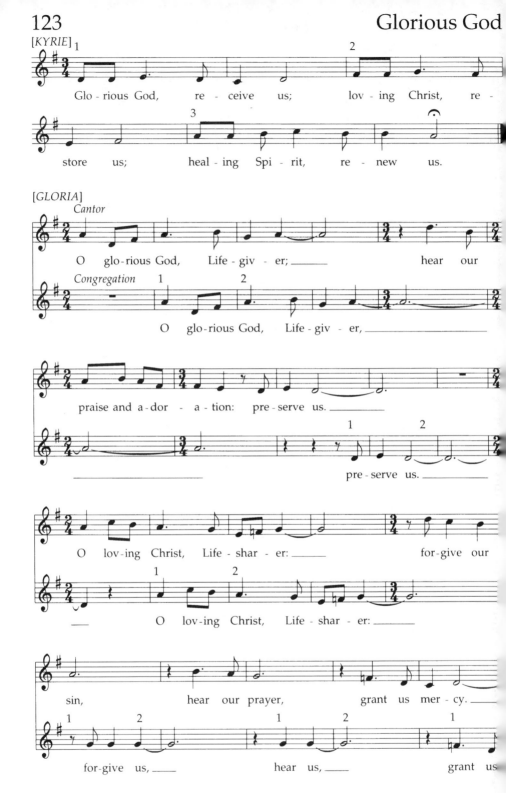

O in-dwell-ing Spi - rit, _____ Life - bear - er: ___

mer - cy. _____ O in-dwell-ing Spi - rit, ___ Life -

_____ reign for - ev - er _____ with our God and

bear - er: ___ reign for - ev - er _____ with our

Christ in ho-ly Trin - i - ty. _____ A - men. _____

God and Christ in ho-ly Trin - i - ty. ___ A - men.

SANCTUS]

Ho - ly, ho - ly, ho - ly un-im-ag-in-a-ble Pow'r:

earth and heav'n sing your praise. O - san - na.

Bless-ings dwell in all who come in your name. O - san - na.

[*AGNUS DEI*]

Lamb, lamb, lamb of God who bears our bur - dens: _____ for - give our sin. _____

Grant us your peace, grant us your peace, grant us your peace.

This is a Mass paraphrase. It should be used at a service other than the principal Eucharist on Sunday. A second or third voice may enter as an echo (like a Round). This echo treatment begins again at the next set of numbers.

Brother, sister, let me serve you

124

Chords: D, G, A7, D, Bm

1 Bro - ther, sis - ter, let me serve you, let me be as
2 We are pil - grims on a jour - ney, fel - low trav'l - lers
3 I will hold the Christ-light for you in the night - time
4 I will weep when you are weep - ing; when you laugh, I'll
5 When we sing to God in hea - ven, we shall find such
6 Bro - ther, sis - ter, let me serve you, let me be as

Chords: Em, A, G, D, G, A7, D

Christ to you; pray that I may have the grace to
on the road; we are here to help each o - ther
of your fear; I will hold my hand out to you,
laugh with you. I will share your joy and sor - row
har - mo - 'ny, born of all we've known to - geth - er
Christ to you; pray that I may have the grace to

Chords: Em, G, A7, D

let you be my ser - vant too.
walk the mile and bear _____ the load.
speak the peace you long _____ to hear.
till we've seen this jour - ney through.
of Christ's love and a - gon - y.
let you be my ser - vant, too.

Capo 2, play D

Words and Music: Richard Gillard; arr. Betty Pulkingham © 1977 Scripture in Song (admin. Integrity Music/ASCAP, c/o Integrity Media, Inc., 1000 Cody Road, Mobile, AL 36695). All rights reserved. Used by permission.

Words: Katharine Hankey (1834-1911).
Music: *Hankey,* William G. Fischer (1835-1910).

1 Thou didst leave thy throne and thy king - ly crown,
2 Hea - ven's arch - es rang when the an - gels sang,
3 The fox - es found rest, and the bird had its nest
4 Thou camest, O Lord, with the liv - ing word
5 When the heavens shall ring, and the an - gels sing,

when thou camest to earth for me;
pro - claim - ing thy royal de - gree;
in the shade of the ce - dar tree;
that should set thy peo - ple free;
at thy com - ing to vic - to - ry,

but in Beth - le - hem's home was there found no room
but in low - ly birth didst thou come to earth,
but thy couch was the sod, O thou son of God,
but with mock - ing scorn and with crown of thorn
let thy voice call me home, say - ing "Yet there is room,

for thy ho - ly na - ti - vi - ty:
and in great hu - mi - li - ty:
in the de - sert of Gal - i - lee:
they bore thee to Cal - va - ry:
there is room at my side for thee:"

O come to my heart, Lord Je - sus;

there is room in my heart for thee.

Words: Emily Elliott (1836-1897).
Music: *Margaret*, T.R. Matthews (1826-1910).

1 Take my yoke u - pon you, all who la - bor long,
2 Come a - way, dis - ci - ple, come, re - treat a - while.
3 Trust - ing and re - turn - ing, you shall grow in strength.
4 When your world is chang - ing at a breath-less pace,
5 When the night grows long - er, and the end is near,

1 I am al - ways with you. Learn my way of liv - ing,
2 I will tra - vel with you, bless - ing de - sert pla - ces,
3 I am al - ways with you, since my love de - signed you,
4 I am al - ways pre - sent, cen - ter in life's turn - ing,
5 I am your com - pan - ion, hope in joy and sor - row,

1 sim - ple and for - giv - ing, and I will give you rest.
2 fill - ing Sab - bath spa - ces, and I will give you rest.
3 seek and I will find you, and I will give you rest.
4 light in la - bor's learn - ing, and I will give you rest.
5 home be - yond to - mor - row, and I will give you rest.

Jesus calls us

1 Je - sus calls us; o'er the tu - mult of our life's wild, rest - less sea, day by day his clear voice sound-eth, say - ing, "Chris - tian, fol - low me;"

2 as, of old, Saint An - drew heard it by the Gal - i - le - an lake, turned from home and toil and kin - dred, leav - ing all for his dear sake.

3 Je - sus calls us from the wor - ship of the vain world's gold - en store; from each i - dol that would keep us, say - ing, "Chris - tian, love me more."

4 In our joys and in our sor - rows, days of toil and hours of ease, still he calls, in cares and plea - sures, "Chris - tian, love me more than these."

5 Je - sus calls us! By thy mer - cies, Sa - vior, may we hear thy call, give our hearts to thine o - be - dience, serve and love thee best of all.

Words: Cecil Frances Alexander (1818-1895).

Music: *Restoration*, melody from *The Southern Harmony*, 1835; harm. *The Hymnal 1982*, after *The Southern Harmony*, 1835.

Jesus calls us

1 Je - sus calls us; o'er the tu - mult of our life's wild,
2 as, of old, Saint An - drew heard it by the Gal - i -
3 Je - sus calls us from the wor - ship of the vain world's
4 In our joys and in our sor - rows, days of toil and
5 Je - sus calls us: by thy mer - cies, Sa - viour, make us

rest - less sea, day by day his sweet voice sound - eth,
le - an lake, turned from home and toil and kin - dred,
gold - en store; from each i - dol that would keep us,
hours of ease, still he calls, in cares and plea - sures,
hear thy call, give our hearts to thine o - be - dience,

say - ing, "Chris - tian, fol - low me;"
leav - ing all for his dear sake.
say - ing, "Chris - tian, love me more."
that we love him more than these.
serve and love thee best of all.

Words: Cecil Frances Alexander (1818-1895).
Music: *St. Andrew*, E.H. Thorne (1834-1916).

I've got a mother in de heaven

130

1 I've got a mo-ther in de heav-en, out - shines de sun,
2 I've got a fa-ther in de heav-en, out - shines de sun,
3 I've got a sis-ter in de heav-en, out - shines de sun,
4 When we get to heav-en, __ we will out - shine de sun,

out - shines de sun, out - shines de sun,
out - shines de sun, out - shines de sun,
out - shines de sun, out - shines de sun,
out - shine de sun, out - shine de sun,

I've got a mo-ther in de heav-en, out - shines de sun,
I've got a fa-ther in de heav-en, out - shines de sun,
I've got a sis-ter in de heav-en, out - shines de sun,
when we get to heav-en, __ we will out - shine de sun,

way be - yond de moon.
way be - yond de moon.
way be - yond de moon.
way be - yond de moon.

Words: Traditional
Music: Negro Spiritual; arr. R. Nathaniel Dett (1882-1943), from *Religious Folk Songs of the Negro As Sung at Hampton Institute* © 1927 Hampton Institute Press (admin. Warner Brothers Publications, Inc., 15800 N.W. 48th Avenue, Box 4340, Miami, FL 33014). All rights reserved. Used by permission.

Lord of all hopefulness

1 Lord of all hope-ful-ness, Lord of all joy,
2 Lord of all ea-ger-ness, Lord of all faith,
3 Lord of all kind-li-ness, Lord of all grace,
4 Lord of all gen-tle-ness, Lord of all calm,

whose trust, ev-er child-like, no cares could des-troy,
whose strong hands were skilled at the plane and the lathe,
your hands swift to wel-come, your arms to em-brace,
whose voice is con-tent-ment, whose pres-ence is balm,

be there at our wak-ing, and give us, we pray,
be there at our la-bors, and give us, we pray,
be there at our hom-ing, and give us, we pray,
be there at our sleep-ing, and give us, we pray,

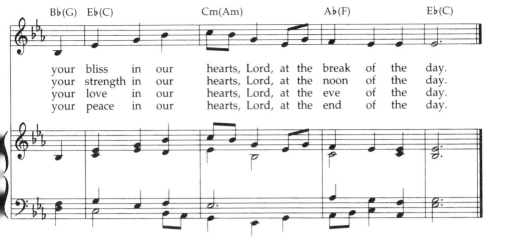

your bliss in our hearts, Lord, at the break of the day.
your strength in our hearts, Lord, at the noon of the day.
your love in our hearts, Lord, at the eve of the day.
your peace in our hearts, Lord, at the end of the day.

Capo 3, play C. Keyboard and guitar should not sound together.

Words: Jan Struther (1901-1953) © Oxford University Press. All rights reserved. Used by permission.
Music: *Slane*, Irish traditional melody; adapt. *The Church Hymnary*, 1927; harm. *The Hymnal 1982*. All rights
        reserved. Used by permission.
You must contact Oxford University Press to reproduce these words.

Take my life

1 Take my life, and let it be con-se-cra-ted, Lord, to thee;
2 Take my voice, and let me sing al-ways, on-ly, for my King;

take my mo-ments and my days, let them flow in cease-less praise.
take my in-tel-lect, and use ev-ery power as thou shalt choose.

Take my hands, and let them move at the im-pulse of thy love;
Take my will, and make it thine; it shall be no long-er mine.

take my heart, it is thine own; it shall be thy roy-al throne.
Take my-self, and I will be ev-er, on-ly, all for thee.

Words: Frances R. Havergal (1836-1879), alt.
Music: *Hollingside*, John Bacchus Dykes (1823-1876).

Take my life

133

1 Take my life and let it be con - se - cra - ted,
2 Take my feet and let them be swift and beau - ti -
3 Take my lips and let them be filled with mes - sa -
4 Take my love, my God, I pour at thy feet its

Lord, to thee; take my hands and let them move
ful for thee; take my voice and let me sing
ges for thee; take my sil - ver and my gold,
treas - ure store; take my - self and I will be

at the im - pulse of thy love, at the im - pulse of thy love.
al - ways, on - ly for my King, al - ways, on - ly for my King.
not a mite would I with - hold, not a mite would I with-hold.
ev - er, on - ly, all for thee, ev - er, on - ly, all for thee.

Words: Frances R. Havergal (1836-1879).
Music: *Hendon*, Henri A. César Malan (1787-1864).

1 Join us, Christian chil - dren help us as we sing
2 Help us, Christian chil - dren lis - ten while we pray
3 Fol - low, Christian chil - dren on our path of love
4 Teach us, Christian chil - dren; seek the Way; be true

of the love of Je - sus let our bright song ring.
"O'er the earth's whole sur - face give us peace to - day,
with the Ho - ly Spi - rit reign-ing from a - bove,
to the love of Je - sus, he who died for you.

Yes, Christ died to save us, died to make us free
strength to do your bid - ding, joy for one and all,
Christ who wept for each of us, saints of long a - go
Find your faith and, do - ing that, lead us, show us, too,

mas - ter as a ser - vant, serve him faith - ful - ly.
God's grace hope and vi - sion wis - dom from the fall."
and, to - day, we, too, the saints, who strive to see, to know.
set us on the Way to Christ: God's Word be - longs to you.

Refrain

Join us, Chris-tian chil - dren help us as we sing

of the love of Je - sus let our bright song ring.

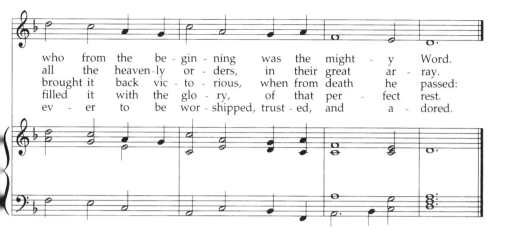

who from the be - gin - ning was the might - y Word.
all the heaven-ly or - ders, in their great ar - ray.
brought it back vic - to - rious, when from death he passed:
filled it with the glo - ry, of that per - fect rest.
ev - er to be wor - shipped, trust - ed, and a - dored.

6 In your hearts enthrone him;
  there let him subdue
  all that is not holy,
  all that is not true:
  crown him as your Captain
  in temptation's hour;
  let his will enfold you
  in its light and power.

7 Surely, this Lord Jesus
  shall return again,
  with his Father's glory,
  with his angel train;
  for all wreaths of empire
  meet upon his brow,
  and our hearts confess him
  King of glory now.

Words: Caroline M. Noel (1817-1877).
Music: *King's Weston*, Ralph Vaughn Williams (1872-1958) © Oxford University Press. All rights reserved.
         Used by permission.
You must contact Oxford University Press to reproduce this music.

136   Mothers, call upon the Maker

She poured the perfume lavishly

1 She poured the per - fume lav - ish - ly, a pound of pre - cious
2 What gift shall I pour out for him who gave his ve - ry

nard, a - noint - ing ten - der - ly the feet that
life? The trea - sure of my heart he seeks, the

nails too soon would pierce. With fra - grance sweet the
pre - cious nard of love. With fra - grance let me

house was filled, with scent of lov - ing deed.
fill his house, with scent of lav - ish love!

I hope my mother will be there

1 I hope my mo - ther will be there, in that beau-ti - ful
2 I hope my sis - ter will be there, in that beau-ti - ful
3 I hope my bro - ther will be there, in that beau-ti - ful
4 I know my Sa - vior will be there, in that beau-ti - ful

world on high, _____ that used to join with
world on high, _____ that used to join with
world on high, _____ that used to join with
world on high, _____ that used to lis - ten

me in pray'r, in that beau-ti - ful world on high.
me in pray'r, in that beau-ti - ful world on high.
me in pray'r, in that beau-ti - ful world on high.
to my pray'r, in that beau-ti - ful world on high.

Refrain

Oh, I will be there, oh I will be there. _____

With the palms of vic - to - ry, crowns of glo - ry you shall wear, in that beau - ti - ful world on high.

Chun-guang ming-mei
Brilliant spring

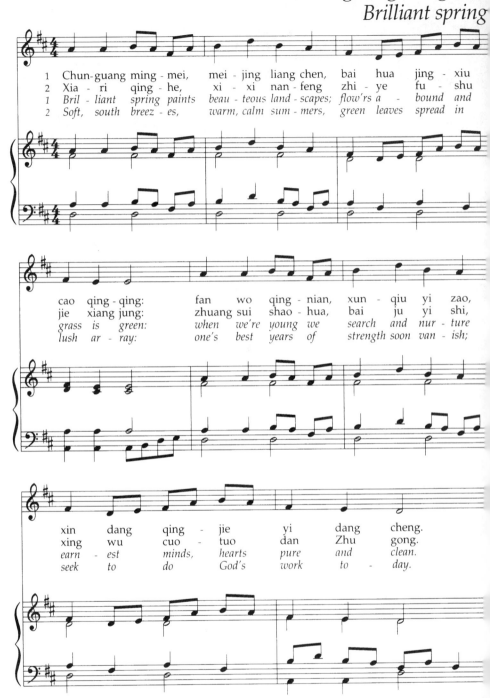

1. Chun-guang ming - mei, mei - jing liang chen, bai hua jing - xiu
2. Xia - ri qing - he, xi - xi nan - feng zhi - ye fu - shu
1. Bril - liant spring paints beau - teous land - scapes; flow'rs a - bound and
2. Soft, south breez - es, warm, calm sum - mers, green leaves spread in

cao qing - qing: fan wo qing - nian, xun - qiu yi zao,
jie xiang jung: zhuang sui shao - hua, bai ju yi shi,
grass is green: when we're young we search and nur - ture
lush ar - ray: one's best years of strength soon van - ish;

xin dang qing - jie yi dang cheng.
xing wu cuo - tuo dan Zhu gong.
earn - est minds, hearts pure and clean.
seek to do God's work to - day.

3. Qiu-guang shuang shi, tian lang qi quig,
    guo-gu feng-ying gong-xian qin:
    wo zhong xian xin, ke zuo hou-ji
    sheng guo hu-yo yu huang-jin.

3. *Autumn's clear days glow with vigor;*
    fruit and grain, earth's yield is made:
    we present our hearts as off'ring,
    these excel gold, pearls and jade.

4. Dong-qi yan-han, xue-hua you qing
    yin chuang shi-jie hie er qing:
    zui-e ban-ban, meng Zhu xi-jing
    yi-shen qing-jie gui tian-cheng.

4. *Snowflakes bring cold winter weather;*
    earth is silv'ry chaste and pure.
    God forgives our sins; this cleans us:
    pure we rise to heaven thus.

Words: Yang Chen-Chang; tr. para. Mildred Wiat and Shiu Tneg-Kiat, alt. © 2002 Baptist Press, Kowloon, Hong Kong. All rights reserved. Used by permission.
Music: *Si-Shi*, Yang Chen-Chang © 2002 Baptist Press, Kowloon, Hong Kong. All rights reserved. Used by permission.

Mandarin pronunciation guide

x = sh   as in   xiu = shoo
                 xun = shun
                 xia = shah
                 xi = shi (shee)
                 xing = shing

q = ch   as in   qiu = choo
                 qi = chi (ee)
                 qing = ching

z = j   as in   Zao = jao
                 zhi = ji (ee)
                 zhu = ju
                 zhaung = jurahng
                 zhong = johng
                 zu-o = ju-o
                 zui-e = ju-e

O perfect love

1 O per-fect love, all hu-man thought tran-scend-ing,
2 O per-fect life, be thou their full as-sur-ance
3 Grant them the joy which bright-ens earth-ly sor-row,

low-ly we kneel in prayer be-fore thy throne,
of tend-er char - i - ty and stead-fast faith
grant them the peace which calms all earth-ly strife;

that theirs may be the love which knows no end - ing, —
of pa - tient hope, and qui - et brave en - dur - ance,
and to life's day the glo - rious un - known mor - row —

whom thou for ev - er - more dost join in one.
with child - like trust that fears nor pain nor death.
that dawns up - on e - ter - nal love and life.

141

Christ, the vine

Christ, the vine, and God, the gard - ener,
we the branch - es bear - ing fruit.
We can bring forth shoots of prom - ise
when our lives in Christ take root.

Christ, the fruit from Jes - se spring - ing,
you ful - filled the pro - phet's trust.
And you pray that we, your bo - dy,
will ful - fill your trust in us.

Words: Edith Sinclair Downing © 1996 Selah Publishing Company, Inc., 58 Pearl Street, P.O. Box 3037, Kingston, NY
         12401. www.selahpub.com. All rights reserved. Used by permission.
Music: *Ecce Deus*, Alfred V. Fedak © 1990 Selah Publishing Company, Inc., 58 Pearl Street, P.O. Box 3037 Kingston,
         NY 12401. www.selahpub.com. All rights reserved. Used by permission.
You must contact Selah Publishing Company to reproduce this selection.

1 Bless now, O God the jour - ney that all your peo - ple make,
2 Bless so - journ-ers and pil - grims who share this wind-ing way—
3 Di - vine e - ter - nal lov - er, you meet us on the road.

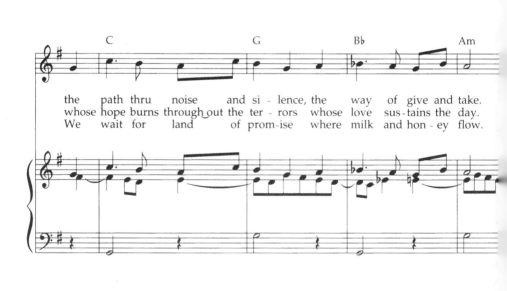

the path thru noise and si - lence, the way of give and take.
whose hope burns through out the ter - rors whose love sus-tains the day.
We wait for land of prom-ise where milk and hon - ey flow.

The trail is found in des-ert and winds the moun-tain round,
We yearn for ho-ly free-dom, while of-ten we are bound.
But wait-ing not for pla-ces— you meet us all a-round.

then leads be-side still wa-ters, the road where faith is found.
To-geth-er we are seek-ing the road where faith is found.
Our cov-e-nant is writ-ten on roads, as faith if found.

found.
found.
found.

Keyboard and guitar should not sound together.

Love astounding

1 Love a - stound-ing, love con - found - ing lim-its fear - ful minds im - pose.
2 Love re - ceiv - ing, love be - liev - ing, we re - joice with thanks and song

Love re - new-ing, love pur - su - ing ev - ery heart un - til it knows
faith re - gain-ing, hope pro - claim-ing; love has taught us, we be - long

love's trans-form-ing, heal - ing good-ness, love's a - bid - ing, gen - tle grace
safe with - in love's tend-er keep-ing, safe from fear's per - sis - tent call.

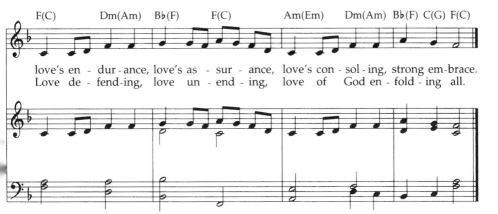

love's en - dur - ance, love's as - sur - ance, love's con - sol - ing, strong em-brace.
Love de - fend-ing, love un - end - ing, love of God en - fold - ing all.

Capo 5, play C

Words: Jeannette M. Lindholm © 1999 Jeannette M. Lindholm. All rights reserved. Used by permission.
Music: *Holy Manna*, from *The Southern Harmony*, 1835; acc. Margaret W. Mealy © Praise Publications. All rights
         reserved. Used by permission.

1 The ser-vants well-pleas-ing to God _____ re-spond with-out
2 The ser-vants well-pleas-ing to God _____ live not for the
3 The ser-vants well-pleas-ing to God _____ know he will sup-

think-ing of self, _____ but joy-ful-ly give from the
praise of the world, _____ but give in re-sponse to God's
ply all their needs; _____ and when they will faith-ful-ly

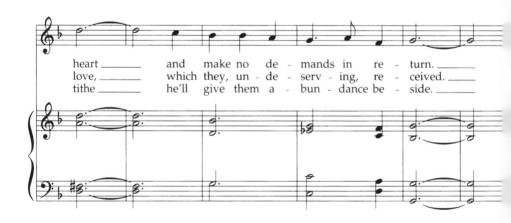

heart _____ and make no de-mands in re-turn. _____
love, _____ which they, un-de-serv-ing, re-ceived. _____
tithe _____ he'll give them a-bun-dance be-side. _____

Refrain

Lord, when did we see you hun-gry, im - pris-oned, lone-ly or

na - ked, in need of a friend? "What-ev - er you've done for

one of these oth - ers, in truth you have done it for me."

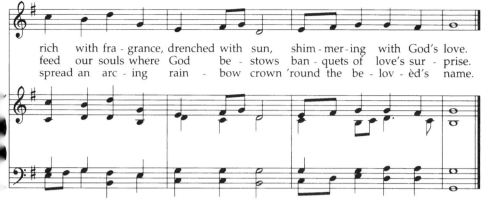

rich   with fra - grance, drenched with sun,   shim - mer - ing   with God's love.
feed   our souls where God   be - stows ban - quets of   love's sur - prise.
spread an   arc - ing   rain -   bow crown 'round the be - lov - èd's   name.

1 Noth-ing dis - tress you,   noth-ing af - fright you
2 Lift your mind up - ward,   fair are his man - sions,
3 See the world's glo - ry!   Fad - ing its splend - our,
4 Love in due mea - sure   mea - sure-less good - ness;
5 Hell may as - sail you,   it can - not move you;

ev - ery - thing pas - ses,   God will a - bide.
noth-ing dis - tress you,   cast fear a - way.
ev - ery - thing pas - ses,   all is de - nied.
pa - tient en - deav - our,   run to love's call!
sor - rows may grieve you,   faith may be tried.

Pa - tient en - deav - our   ac - com-plish-es all things;
Fol - low Christ free - ly,   his love will light you,
Look ev - er home - ward   to the e - ter - nal;
Faith burn-ing bright - ly   be your soul's shel - ter;
Though you have noth - ing,   he is your trea - sure:

who God pos - ses - ses needs naught be - side.
noth-ing af - fright you, in the dark way.
faith - ful in pro - mise God will a - bide.
who hopes, be - liev - ing, ac - com - plishes all.
who God pos - ses - ses needs naught be - side.

Words: Teresa of Avila (1515-1582); tr. Colin P. Thompson © Colin P. Thompson. All rights reserved. Used by
        permission.
Music: *Many Mansions*, Peter Cutts © 1994 Hope Publishing Company, Carol Stream, IL 60188. All rights reserved.
        Used by permission.
You must contact Hope Publishing Company to reproduce this music.

There is a longing in our hearts

Refrain

There is a long-ing in our hearts, O Lord, for

you to re - veal your - self to us.

There is a long-ing in our hearts for love we

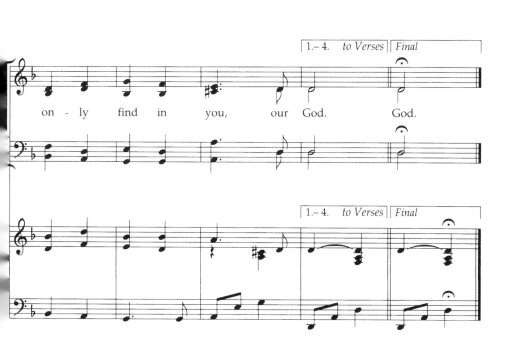

on - ly find in you, our God. God.

1.– 4. *to Verses* | *Final*

1.– 4. *to Verses* | *Final*

1 For jus - tice, for free - dom, for
2 For wis - dom, for cour - age, for
3 For heal - ing, for whole - ness, for
4 Lord save us, take pi - ty, light

mer - cy: hear our prayer. _____ In sor - row,
com - fort: hear our prayer. _____ In weak - ness,
new life: hear our prayer. _____ In sick - ness,
in our dark - ness. _____ We call you,

in grief:
in fear: be near, hear our prayer, O God.
in death:
we wait:

Send out your light

ANTIPHON

Send out your light   and your truth   so   they may lead   me.*

VERSES

1 Give judg - ment for me, O God, and de-fend my cause against an un - godly people;

de - liv - er me from the deceitful and the wick - ed.

2 For you are the   God   of   my   strength;

why   have you put   me   from   you?

Why do I go so heavily while the en-e-my op - pres - ses me?

repeat Antiphon

4 That I may go to the al - tar of God,   to the God of my joy   and glad - ness;

and on the harp I will give thanks to you, O God my God.

repeat Antiphon

5 Why are you so full of heaviness, O my soul?

And why are you so dis-qui - et - ed with - in me?

6 Put your trust in God; for I will yet give thanks to the Most High

who is the help of my cou - te-nance, and my God.

repeat Antiphon

* or F♮

149

I have borrowed him

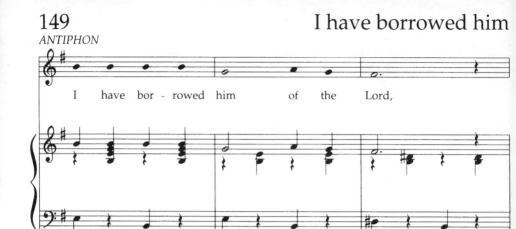

ANTIPHON

I have bor - rowed him of the Lord,

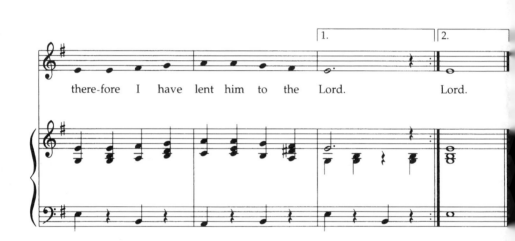

there-fore I have lent him to the Lord.   Lord.

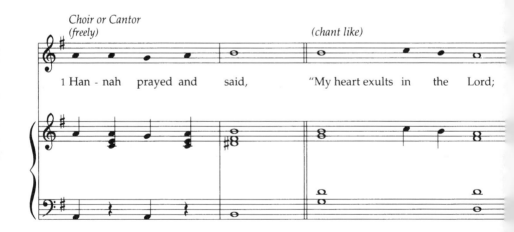

Choir or Cantor
(freely)   *(chant like)*

1 Han - nah prayed and said,   "My heart exults in the Lord;

for the Lord is a God of knowledge, and by him ac - tions are weighed.

4 The bows of the might - y are broken, but the feeble gird on strength.

repeat Antiphon

Choir or Cantor

5 Those who were full have hired themselves out for bread,

but those who were hungry are fat with spoil.

The barren has borne seven, but she who has many child-ren is for-lorn.

6 The Lord kills and brings to life; he brings down to Sheol and rais-es up.

7 The Lord makes poor and makes rich; he brings low, he al-so ex-ults.

8 He raises up the poor from the dust; he lifts the needy from the ash heap,

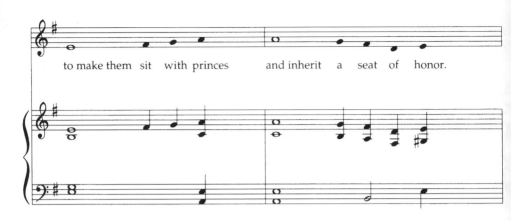

to make them sit with princes and inherit a seat of honor.

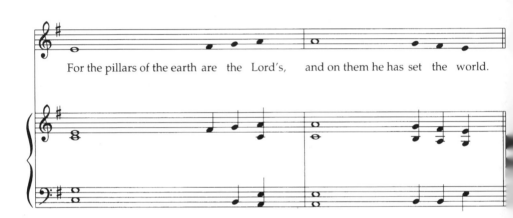

For the pillars of the earth are the Lord's, and on them he has set the world.

repeat Antiphon

Choir or Cantor

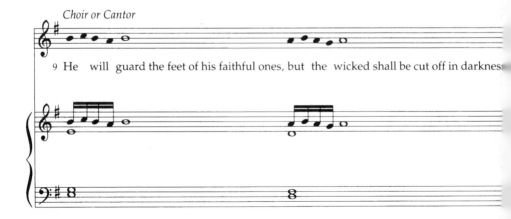

9 He will guard the feet of his faithful ones, but the wicked shall be cut off in darkness.

for not by might does one pre - vail. 10 The Lord! His adversaries shall be shattered;

the Most High will thun - der in heaven. The Lord will judge the ends of the earth,

he will give strength to his king, and exalt the power of his a - nointed."

epeat Antiphon

Declare his glory

De-clare his glo-ry a-mong all   na-tions;   and his won-ders a-mong all   peo-ple.

1.	Sing to the Lord	a	new	song;
2.	Worship the Lord in the beauty of ho	- li -	ness;
3.	Let the heavens rejoice and the	earth	be	glad;
4.	Then shall all the trees	of	the	wood

sing to the   Lord   all   the   earth.
let the whole earth trem - ble   be - fore   him.
let the sea roar and all   that   is   in   it.
shout for   joy   when   he   comes.

Sing to the Lord,   bless   his   name;
Tell it out among the nations: the Lord   is   King;
Let the fields   be   joy - ful,
He shall judge the world with   right - eous - ness,

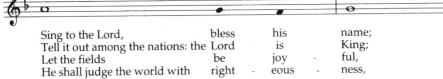

proclaim the good news of his sal-vation   day   by   day.
he will judge the people   with   e - qui - ty.
and all   that   is   there - in.
and the peo   -   ples   with   his   truth.

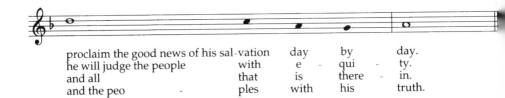

Native American chant style is slow rather than fast. The first line is intoned by a cantor and then repeated by all.
The verses may be sung by a cantor or by all. A hand drum may accompany this chant. It should be played on the
beat throughout in a steady manner with no accents.

Words: Carol Gallagher and Michael Plunkett, para. Psalm 96 of The Book of Common Prayer (1979) of The Episcop.
Church, USA. © 1992 Carol Gallagher and Michael Plunkett. All rights reserved. Used by permission.
Music: Carol Gallagher and Michael Plunkett © 1992 Carol Gallagher and Michael Plunkett. All rights reserved.
Used by permission.

Come, let us sing to the Lord!

Come, let us sing to the Lord! Let us shout for joy to the

rock of our sal - va - tion. Come be-fore his pre - sence with

152

My soul proclaims

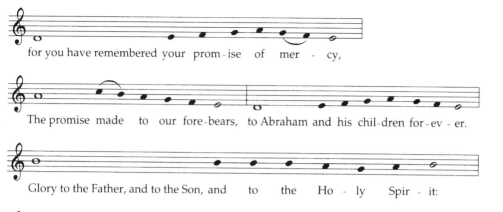

for you have remembered your prom-ise of mer - cy,

The promise made to our fore-bears, to Abraham and his chil-dren for-ev - er.

Glory to the Father, and to the Son, and to the Ho - ly Spir - it:

as it was in the beginning, is now, and will be for - ev - er. A - men.

153
Light of the world

Light of the world in grace and beau-ty;
mir-ror of God's e-ter-nal face;
trans-par-ent flame of love's free du-ty
you bring sal-va-tion to our race.

a tempo

Now, as we see the lights of eve-ning,
we raise our voice in hymns of praise,
wor-thy are you of end-less bless-ing,
sun of our night, lamp of our days.

Words: Phos hilaron, *Enriching Our Worship 1* © 1998 The Church Pension Fund.
Music: Sister Élise, CHS © Community of the Holy Spirit. All rights reserved. Used by permission.

Lord, you now have set your servant free 154

Cantor

Lord, you now have set your ser - vant free

to go in peace as you have prom - ised;

All

For these eyes of mine have seen the Sa - vior,

Cantor

whom you have pre - par - ed for all the world to see:

All

A Light to en-light-en the na-tions, and the glo-ry of your peo - ple Is-ra-el.

Cantor

Glo-ry __ to the Fa - ther, and to the Son, and to the Ho - ly Spir-it:

All

as it was in the be-gin-ning, is now, and will be for-ev - er. A - men.

Words: Nunc dimittis, The Book of Common Prayer (1979) of The Episcopal Church, USA.
Music: Sister Élise, CHS © Community of the Holy Spirit. All rights reserved. Used by permission; ed. CCW
        Sparks © Ralamar Sparks Enterprises. Used by permission. All rights reserved.

Wisdom freed a holy people

1 Wis - dom freed a ho - ly peo - ple, blame - less, from op -
2 Giv - ing them re - ward of la - bors, led the saints a -
3 Through the Red Sea safe - ly brought them, led a - long the
4 For sal - va - tion, Lord, the right - eous praised your name with

pres - sor's sword, and with - stood, with signs and won - ders,
long her way, she was blaze of stars in dark - ness
wat - ers steep, but their en - e - mies she swal - lowed,
one ac - cord: song - filled tongues of new - born peo - ple

ru - lers' dread, to serve the Lord.
and a shel - ter through the day.
o - ver - whelmed them in the deep.
ut - tered Wis - dom's migh - ty word.

Arise and shine

1 A - rise and shine, the pro - phet sang;
2 God's ris - ing sun will light the way,
3 You will not need the sun by day

your light has come, the mes - sage rang.
as peo - ple stream to dawn - ing's ray.
nor moon by night, to light your way;

The shroud of dark - ness stripped a - way,
Your o - pen gates will nev - er close,
God's glo - ry and e - ter - nal might

God's glo - ry brings a bright new day.
in bus' - ling day or night's re - pose.
will be your ev - er - last - ing light.

Words: Patricia B. Clark, para. The Third Song of Isaiah © Gemini Press International. All rights reserved.
Used by permission.

Music: *Wareham*, melody William Knapp (1698-1768), alt.; harm. *Hymns Ancient and Modern*, 1875,
after James Turle (1802-1882).

All you who love Jerusalem

1 All you who love Je - ru - sa - lem, be
2 For God has said, my peace will flow, and
3 Her gen - tle arms will cra - dle you, as

glad and share her cheer. All you who mourn for
trea - sures of the earth. Like banks of wa - ters
mo - ther com - forts child. Your heart will sing as

her sad state will have no cause for fear.
past their fill, her com - fort will pour forth.
you grow strong, like grass - es in the wild.

Words: Patricia B. Clark, para. A Song of Jerusalem Our Mother © Gemini Press International. All rights reserved. Used by permission.
Music: *Edmonton*, from *Harmonica Sacra*, ca. 1760.

I will sing a new song

158

I will sing a new / song to my / God,*
　for you are great and glorious, wonder / ful in / strength, in / vincible.
Let the whole cre / ation / serve you,*
　for you spoke and / all things / came into / being.

You sent your / breath and it / formed them,*
　no one is able / to re / sist your / voice.
Mountains and seas are / stirred to their / depths,*
　rocks / melt like / wax at your / presence.

But to / those who / fear you,*
　you con / tinue / to show / mercy.
No sacrifice, however / fragrant, can / please you,*
　but whoever fears the Lord shall / stand in your / sight for / ever.

God is so good

159

1 God　is　so　good,　God　is　so　good,
2 He　cares　for　me,　he　cares　for　me,
3 He's　all　I　need,　he's　all　I　need,

God　is　so　good,　he's　so　good　to　me.
he　cares　for　me,　he's　so　good　to　me.
he's　all　I　need,　he's　so　good　to　me.

Words:　Traditional
Music:　Negro Spiritual

Thank you, Lord

1 Thank you, Lord, for this fine day, thank you, Lord, for
2 Thank you, Lord, for lov - ing us, thank you, Lord, for
3 Thank you, Lord, for giv-ing us peace, thank you, Lord, for
4 Thank you, Lord, for set-ting us free, thank you, Lord, for

this fine day, thank you, Lord, for this fine day, right where we are.
lov - ing us, thank you, Lord, for lov - ing us, right where we are.
giv-ing us peace, thank you, Lord, for giv-ing us peace, right where we are.
set-ting us free, thank you, Lord, for set-ting us free, right where we are.

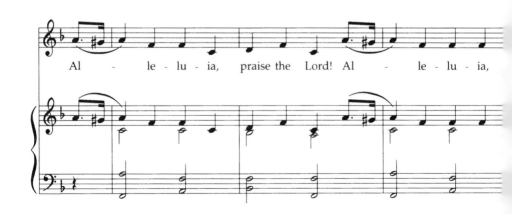

Al - le - lu - ia, praise the Lord! Al - le - lu - ia,

praise the Lord! Al - le - lu - ia, praise the Lord! Right where we are.

loud noise, and re - joice, sing prais - es!

Make a joy - ful noise un - to the Lord. Make a Lord.

162

Rejoice in the Lord always

Re - joice!   Re - joice!   And a - gain I say re - joice!

163

Jesus loves me!

1. Je - sus loves me! this I know, for the bi - ble tells me so;
2. Je - sus loves me! he who died, hea - ven's gate to o - pen wide;
3. Je - sus take this heart of mine, make it pure and whol - ly thine;

lit - tle ones to him be - long; they are weak but he is strong.
he will wash a - way my sin, let his lit - tle child come in.
on the cross you died for me, I will try to live for thee.

Yes, Je - sus loves me! Yes, Je - sus loves me!

Yes, Je - sus loves me! for the bi - ble tells me so.

Words: Anne B. Warner (1820-1915).
Music: William B. Bradbury (1816-1868); arr. Carl Haywood © 2002 Carl Haywood. All rights reserved. Used by
          permission.

The church is wherever God's people are 164

1 The church is wher - ev - er God's peo - ple are prais - ing,
2 The church is wher - ev - er God's peo - ple are help - ing,

sing-ing their thanks for joy on this day. The church is wher-ev-er dis -
car - ing for neigh-bors in sick-ness and need. The church is wher-ev-er God's

ci - ples of Je - sus re - mem-ber his sto - ry and walk in his way.
peo-ple are shar-ing the words of the Bi - ble in gift and in deed.

165

Praise the Lord together

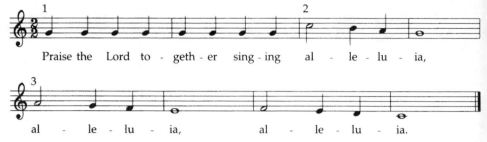

Praise the Lord to - geth - er sing - ing al - le - lu - ia,

al - le - lu - ia, al - le - lu - ia.

Words and Music: Traditional

166

Go now in peace

Go now in peace, go now in peace, may the love of

God sur-round you ev-ery-where, ev-ery-where you may go.

ORFF INSTRUMENT PATTERNS

1 Alto Glockenspiel   2 Metallophone   3 Alto Xylophone   4 Bass Xylophone

The accompaniment may be keyboard, handbells, or Orff instruments.

Words and Music: Natalie Sleeth (1930-1992), from *Sunday Songbook* © 1996 Hinshaw Music, Inc.
All rights reserved. Used by permission.

Indices

Copyrights

Acknowledgment

Every effort has been made to determine the owner and/or administrator of copyrighted material in the book and to obtain the necessary permission. After being given written notice, the publisher will make the necessary correction(s) in subsequent printings.

Permission

The publisher gratefully acknowledges all copyright holders who have permitted the reproduction of their materials in this book. We especially thank those who have consented to allow Church Publishing to issue one-time, not-for-profit use free of charge. **You must contact Church Publishing in writing to obtain this permission** (see address, phone, fax, and email below). Certain selections will note those copyright holder(s) who require that you contact them directly to obtain permission to reprint their materials.

For extended or for-profit use of copyrighted materials in this book, you must write directly to the copyright holder(s). Contact Church Publishing for information. Phone: 1-800-223-6602; Fax: 1-212-779-3392; email: copyrights@cpg.org ; Address: 445 5th Avenue, New York, New York 10016.

American Institute of Musicology
8551 Research Way, Suite 180
Middleton, WI 53562
Phone: 1-608-836-9000
Fax: 1-608-831-8200

Antiochian Orthodox Christian Archdiocese
358 Mountain Road
Englewood, NJ 07631
Phone: 1-201-871-1355
Fax: 1-201-871-7954

Augsburg Fortress Publishers
P.O. Box 1209
Minneapolis, MN 55440-1209
Phone: 1-800-421-0239
Fax: 1-612-330-3252
Email: copyright@augsburgfortress.org

Baptist Press
Administered by the Asian Institute
for Liturgy and Music
Copyrights and Permissions
P.O. Box 3167
Manila 1099
PHILIPPINES
Phone: (011) 632-721-6140
Fax: (011) 632-722-1490
Email: admin@ailm.net

Celebration
Box 309
Aliquippa, PA 15001
Phone: 1-724-375-1501
Fax: 1-724-375-1138

Community of the Holy Spirit
621 West 113th Street
New York, NY 10025-7916
Phone/Fax: 1-212-666-8249

Copyright Company, The
1025 16th Avenue South, Suite 204
Nashville, TN 37212
Phone: 1-615-321-1096
Fax: 1-615-321-1099
Email: tcc@thecopyrightco.com

Crown Publishers
Bonanza Books
A Division of Random House, Inc.
Permissions Department
1745 Broadway
New York, NY 10019
Phone: 1-212-751-2600
Fax: 1-212-572-6066

Editio Musica Budapest
P.O. Box 322
H-1370 Budapest
HUNGARY
Phone: (011) 36-1-4833-100
Fax: (011) 36-1-4833-101
Email: homoloya@emb.hu

EMI Christian Music Publishing
101 Winners Circle
PO Box 5085
Brentwood, TN 37024-5085
Phone: 1-615-371-4400
Fax: 1-615-371-6897

Friedman, Deborah Lynn
Sounds Write Productions, Inc.
6685 Norman Lane
San Diego, CA 92120
Phone: 1-800-9-SOUND-9
Email: www.soundswrite.com

G. Schirmer, Inc.
257 Park Avenue South
New York, NY 10010
Phone: 1-212-254-2100
Fax: 1-212-254-2013
Email: www.schirmer.com

Gemini Press International
14 Forest Row
Great Barrington, MA 01230
Phone: 1-413-528-0905
Fax: 1-413-528-0737
Email: geminipress@earthlink.net

Geneva Press
Administered by Westminster John Knox Press
100 Witherspoon Street
Louisville, KY 40202-1396

GIA Publications, Inc.
7404 S. Mason Avenue
Chicago, IL 60638
Phone: 1-800-GIA-1358
Fax: 1-708-496-3828
Email: www.giamusic.com

Harold Ober Associates, Inc.
425 Madison Avenue
New York, NY 10017
Phone: 1-212-759-8600

Haywood, Carl
5228 Foxboro Landing
Virginia Beach, VA 23464
Email: carlwhaywood@aol.com

Hernández, Ana
157 Wells Street
Peekskill, NY 10566
Phone: 1-914-737-0620
Email: AnaHer@aol.com

Hershey, Sharon Marion
Harvestcross Productions
258 School Lane
Springfield, PA 19064
Phone: 1-610-543-4176

Hinshaw Music, Inc.
P.O. Box 470
Chapel Hill, NC 27514
Phone: 1-919-933-1691
Fax: 1-919-967-3399
Email: www.hinshaw.com

Hope Publishing Company
380 S. Main Place
Carol Stream, IL 60188
Phone: 1-800-323-1049
Fax: 1-630-665-2552
Email: hope@hopepublishing.com

Integrity Music
1000 Cody Road
Mobile, AL 36695-3425
Phone: 1-251-633-9000
Fax: 1-251-776-5036
Email: www.integritymusic.com

Medical Mission Sisters
77 Sherman Street
Hartford, CT 06105
Phone: 1-860-233-0875

MorningStar Music Publishers
1727 Larkin Williams Road
Fenton, MO 63026
Phone: 1-800-647-2117
Fax: 1-636-305-0121

New Song Creations
175 Heggie Lane
Erin, TN 37061
Phone: 1-931-289-3853

Oxford University Press
198 Madison Avenue
New York, NY 10016-4314
Phone: 1-212-726-6000
Fax: 1-212-726-6441
Email: www.oup.com

Oregon Catholic Press
5536 NE Hassalo
Portland, OR 97213-3638
Phone: 1-503-281-1191
Fax: 1-503-282-3486
Email: liturgy@ocp.org

Pilgrim Press
700 Prospect Avenue
Cleveland, OH 44115
Phone: 1-216-736-3764
Fax: 1-216-736-2207
Email: www.pilgrimpress.com

Praise Publications, Inc.
5452 Adele Avenue
Whittier, CA 90601
Phone: (562) 695-1122

Ralamar Sparks Enterprises
6357 Wayne Avenue, #B-5
Philadelphia, PA 19144-3117
Phone: 1-215-842-9687
Fax: 1-215-842-9980
Email: Ralamsen@aol.com

Scripture Union
207-209 Queensway
Bletchley, Milton Keynes
Buckinghamshire MK2 2EB
UNITED KINGDOM
Phone: (011) 44-1908-856-000
Fax: (011) 44-1908-856-111
Email: info@scriptureunion.org.uk

Selah Publishing Company
58 Pearl Street
P.O. Box 3037
Kingston, NY 12402
Phone: 1-845-338-2816
Fax: 1-845-338-2991
Email: www.selahpub.com

Sisters of the Order of St. Benedict
Saint Benedict's Monastery
104 Chapel Lane
St. Joseph, MN 56374-0220
Phone: 1-320-363-7100
Fax: 1-320-363-7130
Email: www.sbm.osb.org

St. Hildegard's Community
7005 Creighton Lane
Austin, TX 78722
Phone: 1-512-926-7500

Sisterhood of St. John the Divine, The
1 Botham Road
Toronto, Ontario M2N 2J5
CANADA
Phone: 1-416-226-2201

Theodore Presser Company
588 N. Gulph Road
King of Prussia, PA 19406-2800
Phone: 1-610-525-3636
Fax: 1-610-527-7841
Email: presser@presser.com

United Methodist Publishing House
201 Eighth Avenue South
P.O. Box 801
Nashville, TN 37202-0801
Phone: 1-615-749-6437
Fax: 1-615-749-6128

Warner Brothers Publications, Inc.
15800 N.W. 48th Avenue, Box 4340
Miami, FL 33014
Phone: 1-305-620-1500
Fax: 1-305-625-3480

Westminster John Knox Press
100 Witherspoon Street
Louisville, KY 40202-1396
Phone: 1-800-277-2872
Fax: 1-502-569-5113
Email: www.ppcpub.com

Index of Authors, Translators, and Sources

Index of Composers, Arrangers, and Sources

Metrical Index of Tunes

87. 87. D
Abbot's Leigh   93
Beach Spring   96
Ecce Deus   4
Holy Manna   87, 143
Rustington   136
Talitha cumi   20
Wellington   116

887.887
Alabaster   1

88. 99
Greensborough   33

888 with Alleluias
O filiie filiae   45

98. 98. 88
Wer nur den lieben Gott   25

99. 9 10
World Wide Communion   85

10. 9. 10. 10
Ferland   114

10 10. 10 10
Slane   21, 131
Via Lucis   78
O quanta qualia   58

11 10 11 10
Highwood   140
Consolation   30

11. 11. 99
Hasting   22
Lourdes   31

11 11 11 11
Anniversary Song   118

Irregular
Beatitude   9
Margaret   126
Robinson Chapel   145
Wilmington   151

Index of Tune Names

Index of First Lines